200 easy suppers

hamlyn | **all colour cookbook**

200 easy suppers

Jo McAuley

An Hachette Livre UK Company

First published in Great Britain in 2008 by
Hamlyn, a division of Octopus Publishing Group Ltd,
2–4 Heron Quays, London E14 4JP
www.octopusbooks.co.uk

ISBN-13: 978-0-600-61729-7

A CIP catalogue record of this book is available from the
British Library.

Printed and bound in China

10 9 8 7 6 5 4 3 2 1

People with known nut allergies should avoid recipes
containing nuts or nut derivatives, and vulnerable people
should avoid dishes containing raw or lightly cooked eggs.

Both metric and imperial measurements are given for
the recipes. Use one set of measurements only, not
a mixture of both.

Standard level spoon measurements are used in all recipes.
1 tablespoon = one 15 ml spoon
1 teaspoon = one 5 ml spoon

Ovens should be preheated to the specified temperature
– if using a fan-assisted oven, follow the manufacturer's
instructions for adjusting the time and the temperature.

Fresh herbs should be used unless otherwise stated.

Medium eggs should be used unless otherwise stated.

Some of the recipes in this book have previously appeared
in the following books published by Hamlyn:
Olive Cookbook by Jo McAuley
Citrus by Jo McAuley
Indoor Grilling by Jo McAuley

contents

introduction

introduction

Being passionate about food and wanting to cook needn't mean spending hours in a hot kitchen, slaving over the stove. No matter how much you enjoy cooking, there is so much else to do and so many other claims on your time that preparing and cooking food sometimes has to come last, and it's all too easy to reach for a ready-made, prepackaged meal from the supermarket shelves.

The recipes in this book show that cooking can be easy. Not all, but most of the recipes take less than 30 minutes to prepare from start to finish, and those that take longer are the kind of recipes you can generally leave to cook away gently so that they'll be ready once you have wound down from the stresses of the day. In general, the ingredients lists are short, the methods minimal and the preparation and cooking times short. This is not to say that the dishes themselves fall below delicious – quite the opposite, in fact.

Experiment

The majority of the recipes serve four as a main course, but many of the salads, soups and vegetarian options would make great starters, when, left as they are, they will comfortably feed eight people. Halve the quantities to serve two. If you are serving a dessert, choose something that can be made in advance, such as a sorbet, or that will cook while you are eating the first course.

Follow the recipes but feel free to alter the quantities or experiment with the choice of ingredients. Cooking should be fun, and even 'easy' doesn't mean that you can't play around and adjust them according to taste.

Healthy eating

A healthy diet is usually a varied diet, and the recipes in this book will help you achieve that without too much hard work or stress. Remember that 'easy' cooking doesn't have to mean reheating a ready-made microwave meal or eating junk food. Just because you don't have a great deal of time, there is no reason to miss out on essential vitamins and minerals and the nutrients that are found in

ingredients such as pulses and lentils. Cooking does not have to be long and complicated to ensure you are receiving all your nutritional needs.

The most important way to make sure that you are maintaining your intake of vitamins and minerals is to buy the freshest possible ingredients. We are all aware that we should aim for five daily portions of fruit and vegetables, but don't forget that frozen produce often has an equal, sometimes even a higher, nutritional value to fresh as long as it is processed immediately after picking.

Being prepared

We are told all the time how important it is to shop wisely. This is never more true than when you are aiming to cook simple, quick dishes, where each ingredient is of the utmost importance. For example, a fantastic olive oil or organic wild salmon fillet can make the difference between a dish that is merely acceptable and one that tastes wonderful. Many of the recipes in this book have one or two strong flavours, which serve to bring the dish to life. It's amazing how the zestiness of a lemon or the perfume of a few sage leaves can transform a meal. Fresh herbs, good-quality ingredients and a great combination of flavours and textures mean that easy cooking does not mean boring eating.

Don't feel guilty about making life a little easier and making the most of the great-quality, ready-made time-savers that are so readily available to us today. When you are shopping, look out for jars of pesto and tapenades, cooked rice, lentils and pulses, deli-style roast vegetables. Look out, too, for jars of ready-minced garlic and ginger, which are now widely available in supermarkets and which mean that you can add the wonderful flavours without having to spend time peeling, crushing and grating. Don't forget that you can also buy pre-cut strips of meat, such as beef or pork, which is perfect for stir-fries. Frozen pastry is essential for anyone wanting to cook easy pies or tarts: just remember to take it out of the freezer in good time to thaw before you start cooking.

Store-cupboard essentials

One of the best ways of making life easy in the kitchen is to have a well-stocked store cupboard and freezer, so you need to buy just one or two items – fresh fish or meat or some seasonal vegetables – and combine them with staples such as rice and noodles and some well-flavoured spices or ready-made sauces.

Pulses, lentils & beans

Cans of precooked beans and lentils can be quickly heated through to make a simple meal substantial and filling. Experiment with different types. For example, borlotti beans are pretty and speckled when dried and light brown once cooked. Cannellini beans are a similar size to kidney beans but pale in colour.

Puy lentils are small, round, flattish lentils, slate grey in colour, and they are widely agreed to be the best of lentils because of their slightly peppery taste and the fact that they will hold their shape and slight bite during cooking, making them more robust than most lentils. They are available ready-cooked or dried in most good supermarkets.

Pasta, noodles, grains & rice

Pasta takes little time to cook and can be used to accompany a wide range of dishes. Rice takes longer to cook, but it is possible to buy precooked rice. Cellophane, rice and udon noodles take just a few minutes to prepare and can be added to soups and stir-fries to create filling, nourishing dishes.

Less often used, but just as useful for the easy cook, is wild rice. It is actually a kind of grass and is very hard, so it needs to be cooked for longer than white rice – but it has a delicious, slightly nutty flavour. Wild rice tends to be more expensive than white and brown rices and so is often mixed with white rice to reduce the cost yet retain its taste.

You should also experiment with quinoa, a protein-rich grain that is light and tasty and which can be used as a side dish or part of a main course, or added to soups, salads or starters and even desserts and cakes.

Polenta, an Italian cornmeal made from maize, takes about 40 minutes to cook from scratch, but it is also available in precooked form, which will only take a few minutes to prepare, or as firm polenta, which has been cooked and usually baked in rectangles so that it can be sliced and fried in oil.

Herbs & spices

Make sure your shelves are well stocked with spices and herbs. It is also easy to keep a few herbs – basil, parsley and coriander – growing on the kitchen windowsill, so that you can add a few freshly chopped leaves to garnish finished dishes.

Thai basil is very different from the more familiar herb we tend to use. It has dark green leaves and purplish stems and flowers, and its flavours are sweet, pungent and slightly aniseed. It is used throughout Thailand and beyond in stir-fries and salads. It is possible to buy it fresh, and some good supermarkets also stock Thai basil in jars.

Most large supermarkets and specialist stores stock other prepared spices that will bring novel and interesting flavours to your easy dishes. Ras el hanout is a blend of up to 21 spices used in Middle Eastern and North African cooking. Chinese five spice combines equal parts of star anise, Szechwan pepper, fennel, ground cinnamon and cloves. Garam masala is a blend of ground spices, popular in Indian cooking, that is generally used at the end of cooking, stirred in just before serving to round off the flavours of the dish.

Sumac is the ground version of berries grown and dried around the Mediterranean and is used frequently in Greek and Turkish cooking. It has a tart, sour lemon taste. If you cannot get hold of sumac, grated lemon rind can be used instead.

Sauces & pastes

If you like to experiment with Eastern dishes, you will probably already have jars of Thai red and green sauces and bottles of soy sauce on your shelves.

Some of recipes in this book include teriyaki sauce. Of course, you can make your own by heating soy, mirin, sugar and sake together and bubbling until thickened. Otherwise, buy it ready-made from any supermarket or Asian food shop.

Tahini is a thick paste made from hulled, roasted sesame seeds, and it is a key ingredient in hummus. You will find tahini in most supermarkets or Middle Eastern food stores.

Harissa is a very hot, North African smoked chilli pepper paste. It is widely used in Moroccan and Tunisian cooking and is often served with couscous or as condiment with grilled meats and fish.

meat

butter bean & bacon soup

Serves **4**
Preparation time **15 minutes**
Cooking time **24 minutes**

2 tablespoons **olive oil**
175 g (6 oz) **smoked bacon**, chopped
25 g (1 oz) **butter**
1 **onion**, chopped
2 **garlic cloves**, roughly chopped
2 **celery sticks**, chopped
1 **leek**, roughly chopped
750 ml (1¼ pints) hot **ham** or **vegetable stock**
400 g (13 oz) can **butter beans**, drained and rinsed
2 large sprigs of **parsley**
3 sprigs of **thyme**
2 **bay leaves**
100 ml (3½ fl oz) **double cream**
salt and **pepper**

Heat 1 tablespoon of the oil in a large pan and fry the bacon until it is crisp and golden. Remove with a slotted spoon and set aside to drain on kitchen paper.

Melt the butter and remaining oil in the pan over a medium heat and cook the onion, garlic, celery and leek, stirring frequently, for about 10 minutes or until soft and golden.

Add the stock and butter beans with the herbs and season to taste. Bring to the boil, then turn the heat down and simmer gently for about 10 minutes before removing from the heat. Remove the herbs and blend until smooth.

Stir in the cream, season to taste and serve in large bowls, scattered with crispy bacon.

For smoked sausage & borlotti bean soup, replace the smoked bacon with 250 g (8 oz) smoked pork sausage and use a 400 g (13 oz) can of borlotti beans instead of the butter beans. Omit the cream.

pan-fried liver & bacon salad

Serves **4**
Preparation time **10 minutes**
Cooking time **8–12 minutes**

6 tablespoons **olive oil**
375 g (12 oz) **calves' liver**,
   dusted with **seasoned flour**
250 g (8 oz) cooked **new
   potatoes**, sliced
200 g (7 oz) **streaky bacon**,
   sliced
3 **shallots**, sliced
2 tablespoons **raspberry
   vinegar**
1 tablespoon **wholegrain
   mustard**
1 head **frisée**, leaves
   separated
salt and **pepper**

Heat 2 tablespoons of the oil in a frying pan. Fry the floured liver for 1–2 minutes on each side. Lift on to kitchen paper and keep warm.

Add 1 tablespoon of the oil to the pan and fry the potato slices, turning occasionally, for 4–5 minutes or until crisp and golden. Lift on to kitchen paper and keep warm with the liver.

Add 1 tablespoon of the oil to the pan and fry the bacon for 2–3 minutes before adding the shallots. Cook until soft and golden.

Mix together the raspberry vinegar, mustard and remaining oil.

Arrange the salad leaves on serving plates and pile on the potatoes, bacon and shallots. Slice the liver thinly before arranging on each salad, drizzle over the dressing and serve.

For chicken liver, mushroom & bacon salad, omit the calves' livers and start by frying the potatoes, as above. When adding the shallots to the bacon, also add 100 g (3½ oz) button mushrooms. Lastly, fry 375 g (12 oz) diced chicken livers. Arrange as above.

thai beef salad

Serves **4**

Preparation time **15 minutes**, plus standing

Cooking time **6–8 minutes**

2 lean rump or sirloin **steaks**, about 150 g (5 oz) each, trimmed

150 g (5 oz) **baby sweetcorn**

1 large **cucumber**

1 small **red onion**, finely chopped

3 tablespoons chopped **coriander**

4 tablespoons **rice wine vinegar**

4 tablespoons **sweet chilli dipping sauce**

2 tablespoons **sesame seeds**, lightly toasted, to garnish

Put the steaks in a preheated hot griddle pan and cook for 3–4 minutes on each side. Allow to rest for 10–15 minutes, then slice the meat thinly.

Meanwhile, cook the sweetcorn in boiling water for 3–4 minutes or until tender. Refresh under cold water and drain well.

Slice the cucumber in half lengthways, then scoop out and discard the seeds. Cut the cucumber into 5 mm (¼ inch) slices.

Put the beef, sweetcorn, cucumber, onion and chopped coriander in a large bowl. Stir in the vinegar and chilli sauce and mix well. Garnish the salad with sesame seeds and serve.

For Thai tofu salad, omit the steaks and cube 500 g (1 lb) firm tofu. Griddle for 2–3 minutes on each side until hot and golden. Mix with the other ingredients and garnish, as above.

individual italian fillet steak parcels

Serves **4**
Preparation time **10 minutes**
Cooking time **20 minutes**

1 tablespoon **olive oil**
4 **fillet steaks**, about 150 g
(5 oz) each
8 large squares of **filo pastry**
150 g (5 oz) **butter**, melted
125 g (4 oz) **buffalo**
mozzarella cheese, cut into
4 slices
2 teaspoons chopped
marjoram
2 teaspoons chopped
oregano
4 **sun-blushed tomatoes**,
shredded
2 tablespoons finely grated
Parmesan cheese
salt and **pepper**

Salad
150 g (5 oz) **rocket**
125 g (4 oz) **buffalo**
mozzarella cheese, cubed
½ **red onion**, finely sliced
(optional)
2 ripe **plum tomatoes**, sliced

Heat the oil in a hot frying pan and sear the steaks for
2 minutes on each side (they will continue cooking in
the oven). Remove and set aside.

Brush each sheet of pastry with melted butter and
arrange 2 sheets on a work surface. Place a steak
in the centre of the pastry, followed by a slice of
mozzarella, one-quarter of the herbs and sun-blushed
tomato shreds. Season and bring up the sides of the
pastry. Scrunch it together at the top to seal the steak
into a parcel. Sprinkle over one-quarter of the grated
Parmesan. Repeat with the remaining steaks.

Cook in a preheated oven, 220°C (425°F), Gas Mark 7,
for 15 minutes until the pastry is crisp and golden
brown. Remove and leave to rest for 2–3 minutes.

Toss the salad ingredients together, season and serve
with the parcels.

For summertime chicken parcels, use 4 chicken
breasts instead of the steaks – you will need to fry
them for about 5 minutes on each side. For a stronger
flavour, replace the toppings with either 125 g (4 oz)
sliced Gorgonzola, 25 g (1 oz) roughly chopped
walnuts and 2 tablespoons roughly chopped chives or
125 g (4 oz) sliced firm goats' cheese, 25 g (1 oz)
black pitted olives and 2 tablespoons shredded basil.

malay beef with peanut sauce

Serves **4**
Preparation time **10 minutes**
Cooking time **15 minutes**

500 g (1 lb) sirloin or rump
   steak, thinly sliced
1 tablespoon **vegetable oil**

Marinade
½ teaspoon **turmeric**
1 teaspoon **ground cumin**
½ teaspoon **fennel seeds**
1 **bay leaf**, finely shredded
½ teaspoon **ground cinnamon**
75 ml (3 fl oz) **coconut cream**

Rice
250 g (8 oz) **Thai jasmine
   rice**
200 ml (7 fl oz) **coconut milk**
½ teaspoon **salt**

Peanut sauce
2 tablespoons **crunchy
   peanut butter**
¼ teaspoon **cayenne pepper**
1 tablespoon **light soy sauce**
125 ml (4 fl oz) **coconut
   cream**
½ teaspoon **caster sugar**

Make the marinade by mixing together all the ingredients in a non-metallic bowl. Add the beef, mix thoroughly, then thread the beef on to skewers and set aside to marinate.

Put the rice, coconut milk, salt and 250 ml (8 fl oz) water in a rice cooker or a covered saucepan over a low heat. Cook for about 15 minutes until the rice is cooked and the liquid has been absorbed.

Meanwhile, add the ingredients for the peanut sauce to a small saucepan with 3 tablespoons water and heat gently, stirring.

Heat the oil in a large frying pan and cook the beef skewers for about 5 minutes, turning so that each side is browned evenly. Serve immediately with the rice and peanut sauce.

For bean sprout & carrot salad to serve as an accompaniment, coarsely grate 4 carrots, roughly chop 4 spring onions and combine with 200 g (7 oz) bean sprouts.

lamb chops with olive couscous

Serves **4**

Preparation time **25 minutes**,
plus marinating

Cooking time **10–12 minutes**

6 **anchovy fillets in olive oil**,
drained and chopped

2 tablespoons **black olive
tapenade**

2–3 sprigs of **thyme**, leaves
stripped and chopped

1 sprig of **rosemary**, leaves
stripped and chopped

2 **bay leaves**, torn

2–3 **garlic cloves**, crushed

finely grated rind of **1 lemon**

4 tablespoons **white wine**

125 ml (4 fl oz) **olive oil**

4 **lamb loin chops**, about
150 g (5 oz) each

300 g (10 oz) **medium-grain
couscous**

2 tablespoons **salted capers**
or **capers in brine**, drained
and rinsed

100 g (3½ oz) **spicy-marinated
green olives**, chopped

75 g (3 oz) **wild rocket
leaves**, plus extra for serving

4 tablespoons **lemon juice**,
plus extra for serving

salt and **pepper**

Mash the anchovies with a fork and stir them into a
bowl with the tapenade. Add the herbs, garlic and
lemon rind, then pour in the wine and 4 tablespoons
of the oil. Stir thoroughly, then rub the mixture into the
lamb chops. Cover and leave at room temperature for
about 1 hour.

Put the couscous into a heatproof bowl and stir in
2 tablespoons of the oil so that the grains are covered.
Season with salt and pour over 400 ml (14 fl oz)
boiling water. Leave to stand for 5–8 minutes until
the grains are soft.

Season the lamb chops with pepper and cook them
for about 2 minutes in a preheated hot griddle pan.
Sprinkle with a little salt, then cook the other side
for a further 2 minutes. Transfer to a warm dish, cover
with foil and leave to rest for 5 minutes.

Fluff up the couscous with a fork and gently fold in
the capers, olives and rocket. Sprinkle over the lemon
juice, then heap the couscous on to warm plates.
Arrange a lamb chop on each heap and spoon over
the juices. Sprinkle with rocket leaves, drizzle with the
remaining oil and an extra squeeze of lemon juice and
serve immediately with lemon wedges.

For stir-fried lamb, heat 1½ tablespoons vegetable
oil in a wok and cook 250 g (8 oz) fillet of lamb, thinly
sliced, for a few minutes. Add 1 tablespoon each
oyster sauce and Thai fish sauce, 1 crushed garlic
clove and 1 tablespoon finely sliced red chilli and
cook for a further 2 minutes. Garnish with mint leaves.

sri lankan-style lamb curry

Serves **4**
Preparation time **10 minutes**
Cooking time **28–33 minutes**

500 g (1 lb) **shoulder** or **leg
of lamb**, diced
2 **potatoes**, peeled and cut
into large chunks
4 tablespoons **olive oil**
400 g (13 oz) can **chopped
tomatoes**
salt and **pepper**

Curry paste
1 **onion**, grated
1 tablespoon finely chopped
fresh **root ginger**
1 teaspoon finely chopped
garlic
½ teaspoon **turmeric**
1 teaspoon **ground coriander**
½ teaspoon **ground cumin**
½ teaspoon **fennel seeds**
½ teaspoon **cumin seeds**
3 **cardamom pods**, lightly
crushed
2 **green chillies**, finely
chopped
5 cm (2 inch) **cinnamon stick**
2 **lemon grass stalks**, finely
sliced

Make the curry paste by mixing together all the
ingredients in a large bowl – for a milder curry remove
the seeds from the chillies before chopping them finely.
Add the lamb and potatoes and combine well.

Heat the oil in a heavy-based pan or casserole and tip
in the meat and potatoes. Use a wooden spoon to stir-
fry for 6–8 minutes. Pour in the chopped tomatoes and
150 ml (¼ pint) water, bring to the boil and season well
then allow to bubble gently for 20–25 minutes until the
potatoes are cooked and the lamb is tender.

Serve accompanied with toasted naan bread and a
bowl of Greek yogurt, if liked.

For beef & potato curry, use 500 g (1 lb) diced rump
steak instead of the lamb. Prepare it in the same way
as the lamb, then serve it with a generous sprinkling of
chopped coriander.

lamb with rosemary oil

Serves **4**
Preparation time **10 minutes**
Cooking time **10–20 minutes**

about 750 g (1½ lb) **lamb loin
  roast**, trimmed of fat
4 **garlic cloves**, cut into slivers
a few small sprigs of
  rosemary
2 **red onions**, quartered
50 ml (2 fl oz) **olive oil**
1 tablespoon chopped
  rosemary
salt and **pepper**

Make small incisions all over the lamb loin and insert the garlic slivers and rosemary sprigs.

Place the meat in a preheated hot griddle pan and cook, turning occasionally, until seared all over for about 10 minutes for rare or about 20 minutes for well done.

Add the onions half-way through the cooking time and char on the outside. Let the lamb rest for 5 minutes, then carve into slices.

Meanwhile, put the oil and rosemary in a mortar and crush with a pestle to release the flavours. Season with salt and pepper.

Spoon the rosemary oil over the lamb slices and serve at once with the fried onions.

Serve with fresh pasta, lightly tossed in oil, and Parmesan shavings.

For lamb chops with garlic & herbs, cut 4 garlic cloves into slivers and insert into incisions in 8 lamb chops. Place each chop on a square of foil and divide 50 g (2 oz) butter, 3 tablespoons lemon juice and 1 tablespoon each dried oregano and dried mint among them. Season and fold the foil to encase the meat. Cook in a preheated oven, 180°C (350°F), Gas Mark 4, for 1½–2 hours.

taverna-style grilled lamb with feta

Serves **4**
Preparation time **8 minutes**
Cooking time **6–8 minutes**

500 g (1 lb) leg or **shoulder of lamb**, diced

Marinade
2 tablespoons chopped
  oregano
1 tablespoon chopped
  rosemary
grated rind of 1 **lemon**
2 tablespoons **olive oil**
salt and **pepper**

Feta salad
200 g (7 oz) **feta cheese**,
  sliced
1 tablespoon chopped
  oregano
2 tablespoons chopped
  parsley
grated rind and juice of
  1 **lemon**
½ small **red onion**, finely sliced
3 tablespoons **olive oil**

Mix together the marinade ingredients in a non-metallic bowl, add the lamb and mix to coat thoroughly. Thread the meat on to 4 skewers.

Arrange the sliced feta on a large serving dish and sprinkle over the herbs, lemon rind and sliced onion. Drizzle over the lemon juice and oil and season with salt and pepper.

Cook the lamb skewers under a preheated hot grill or in a griddle pan for about 6–8 minutes, turning frequently until browned and almost cooked through. Remove from heat and leave to rest for 1–2 minutes.

Serve the lamb, with any pan juices poured over, with the salad and accompanied with plenty of crusty bread, if liked.

For pork with red cabbage, replace the lamb with the same quantity of lean, boneless pork. Marinate and cook the pork as above. Replace the feta with 250 g (8 oz) finely chopped red cabbage. Omit the oregano and swap the lemon for an orange. Mix the ingredients together and marinate for 5 minutes before serving.

fragrant lamb cutlets

Serves **4**

Preparation time **5 minutes**,
plus marinating

Cooking time **15 minutes**

12 **lamb cutlets**

4 **sweet potatoes**, baked
in their skins

salt and **pepper**

rocket leaves, to serve

Marinade

finely grated rind and juice
of ½ **lemon**

2 **garlic cloves**, crushed

2 tablespoons **olive oil**, plus
extra for brushing

4 sprigs of **rosemary**, finely
chopped

4 **anchovy fillets in olive oil**,
drained and finely chopped

2 tablespoons **lemon cordial**

Mix together all the marinade ingredients in a non-metallic bowl, then add the lamb cutlets. Season to taste with salt and pepper, turn the cutlets to coat and set aside for 15 minutes to marinate.

Cook the cutlets under a preheated hot grill for 3–5 minutes on each side or until slightly charred and cooked through. Keep warm and allow to rest.

Meanwhile, cut the baked sweet potatoes into quarters, scoop out some of the flesh and brush the skins with oil. Season to taste with salt and pepper and cook for about 15 minutes under the grill until crisp. Serve with the lamb cutlets and rocket leaves.

For pork patties with sweet potato slices, mix 500 g (1 lb) minced pork with the marinade ingredients, omitting the anchovies. Using your hands, form the mince mixture into little patties and cook under a hot grill for 5–6 minutes on each side until browned and cooked through. Serve with sweet potato skins and rocket leaves, as above.

pork fillet with mushrooms

Serves **4**
Preparation time **15 minutes**
Cooking time **15–17 minutes**

4 tablespoons **olive oil**
500 g (1 lb) **pork tenderloin**,
   sliced into 5 mm (¼ inch)
   discs
300 g (10 oz) **mushrooms**,
   trimmed and cut into chunks
1 **lemon**
300 ml (½ pint) **crème fraîche**
2 sprigs of **tarragon**, leaves
   stripped
salt and **pepper**

Heat 2 tablespoons of the oil in the pan over a
medium-high heat and fry the pork slices for
3–4 minutes, turning once so that they are browned
on both sides. Remove with a slotted spoon.

Add the remaining oil to the pan, tip in the mushrooms
and cook for 3–4 minutes, stirring occasionally, until
softened and golden.

Cut half of the lemon into slices and add to the pan
to brown a little on each side, then remove and
set aside.

Return the pork to the pan, add the crème fraîche and
tarragon and pour in the juice from the remaining
lemon. Season well, bring to the boil, then reduce the
heat and leave to bubble gently for 5 minutes. Add
the prepared lemon slices at the last minute and gently
stir through.

Serve the pork with white rice or crispy potato wedges.

For couscous with petit pois to serve as an
accompaniment, soak 250 g (8 oz) couscous in
400 ml (14 fl oz) just-boiled water or vegetable stock
and leave for 5–8 minutes until soft. Fluff up the
couscous with a fork and season. Boil 150 g (5 oz)
frozen petit pois for 3 minutes, drain, then mix them
with the couscous. Before serving, add a handful of
chopped chives, a few knobs of butter and season
with black pepper.

pork in cider with pappardelle

Serves **4**

Preparation time **8 minutes**

Cooking time **20 minutes**

15 g (½ oz) **dried wild mushrooms**

3 tablespoons **olive oil**

400 g (13 oz) boneless **pork loin steaks**

150 g (5 oz) **smoked bacon**, sliced

8 **shallots**, quartered

300 ml (½ pint) **dry cider**

125 ml (4 fl oz) **cider vinegar**

2 sprigs of **thyme**

1 **bay leaf**, torn

400 g (13 oz) fresh **pappardelle** or thick ribbon pasta

200 ml (7 fl oz) **crème fraîche**

salt and **pepper**

Soak the dried mushrooms for 5–10 minutes in 6 tablespoons boiling water.

Meanwhile, heat the oil in a large frying pan over a medium heat and fry the pork and bacon for approximately 3 minutes until browned. Add the shallots and continue frying for a further 2–3 minutes until golden and beginning to soften.

Pour in the dry cider and cider vinegar and add the mushrooms and soaking liquid. Stir in the herbs and season well. Bring to the boil, then reduce the heat, cover and leave to bubble gently for 10–12 minutes until the shallots are soft.

Meanwhile, cook the pasta in lightly salted boiling water for 3 minutes or according to the instructions on the packet. Drain and transfer to serving dishes.

Stir the crème fraîche into the pork, increase the heat briefly and then place the meat on the pasta and spoon over the sauce. Serve immediately.

For venison in red wine, substitute the pork for 4 venison steaks cut into strips and replace the cider with red wine. Omit the cider vinegar. Serve as above.

crispy parma ham parcels

Serves **4**

Preparation time **10 minutes**

Cooking time **4 minutes**

8 slices of **Parma ham** or
   prosciutto

100 g (3½ oz) creamy
   blue cheese, such as
   Roquefort, St Agur,
   dolcelatte or Gorgonzola,
   thinly sliced

1 teaspoon chopped **thyme
   leaves**

1 **pear**, peeled, cored and
   diced

25 g (1 oz) **walnuts**, chopped

To serve

watercress leaves tossed in
   olive oil and **balsamic
   vinegar**

1 **pear**, peeled, cored and
   sliced

Put a slice of Parma ham on a chopping board and
then put a second slice across it to form a cross shape.

Arrange one quarter of the cheese slices in the centre,
scatter over some thyme and top with one quarter of
the diced pear.

Add one quarter of the walnuts, then fold over the
sides of the ham to form a neat parcel. Repeat this
process to make 4 parcels.

Transfer the parcels to a foil-lined grill pan and cook
under a preheated hot grill for about 2 minutes on
each side until the ham is crisp and the cheese is
beginning to ooze out of the sides.

Serve the parcels immediately with the dressed
watercress leaves and slices of pear.

For figs with Parma ham, quarter 8 fresh figs, leaving
them attached at the base. Mix 1 teaspoon Dijon
mustard with 125 g (4 oz) ricotta cheese, season to
taste and spoon over the figs. Divide 85 g (3¼ oz)
Parma ham, cut into strips, among them and drizzle
over 2 tablespoons balsamic vinegar.

pork chops with lemon & thyme

Serves **4**
Preparation time **20 minutes**
Cooking time **28–30 minutes**

finely grated rind of 1 **lemon**
1 tablespoon chopped **thyme**
2 tablespoons **olive oil**
2 **garlic cloves**, crushed
4 **pork chops**, about 200 g
   (7 oz) each
1 kg (2 lb) **floury potatoes**,
   peeled and quartered
200 ml (7 fl oz) **double cream**
50 g (2 oz) **butter**
salt and **pepper**
thyme, leaves or flowers,
   to garnish

Mix together the lemon rind, thyme, oil, garlic and
plenty of pepper and rub the mixture over the pork
chops. Set aside.

Meanwhile, cook the potatoes in lightly salted boiling
water for about 20 minutes or until soft. Drain, return
to the pan and mash. Add the cream, butter and
seasoning and use a electric hand-held whisk to beat
until smooth.

Heat a dry frying pan over a medium-high heat and
cook the pork chops for 4–5 minutes on each side,
depending on their thickness, until cooked and golden.

Remove the pork from the heat and leave to rest for
1–2 minutes before serving garnished with a few thyme
leaves or flowers and accompanied by the fluffy mash.

For spinach & Parmesan mash instead of plain
mash, cook, drain and chop 500 g (1 lb) spinach.
Mash the potatoes with butter and milk (omit the
cream) and stir in the spinach and 50 g (2 oz) freshly
grated Parmesan.

pork with aubergine & noodles

Serves **4**
Preparation time **15 minutes**
Cooking time **15 minutes**

500 g (1 lb) **minced pork**
250 g (8 oz) **thick, flat rice
noodles**
about 3 tablespoons
vegetable or **groundnut oil**
1 large **aubergine**, cut into
1 cm (½ inch) dice
2 tablespoons **coriander
leaves**, plus extra to garnish

Marinade
1 tablespoon **dark soy sauce**
3 tablespoons **light soy
sauce**, plus extra to serve
(optional)
1 tablespoon **cornflour**
1 teaspoon **clear honey**
1 tablespoon **chilli paste**
2 teaspoons finely chopped
garlic
1 tablespoon finely chopped
root ginger

Make the marinade by mixing together all the
ingredients in a non-metallic bowl. Add the pork and
combine thoroughly until the liquid has been absorbed.
Set aside.

Cook the noodles in boiling water for 2–3 minutes or
according to the instructions on the packet. Drain.

Heat the oil until smoking in a large wok or frying pan.
Carefully stir-fry the aubergine until golden and soft.
Remove with a slotted spoon and leave to drain on
kitchen paper.

Add more oil to the pan if necessary and stir-fry the
pork until browned and cooked through. Pour in 75 ml
(3 fl oz) water and allow to gently bubble. Return the
aubergine to the wok and heat through, then add
the coriander leaves.

Serve the pork and aubergine piled on top of the
noodles and with a scattering of coriander leaves and
some extra light soy sauce, if liked.

For minced steak with okra & rice, cook 250 g
(8 oz) rice instead of noodles and substitute the
minced pork with the same quantity of minced steak.
Replace the aubergine with 200 g (7 oz) okra, sliced
into 1 cm (½ inch) pieces and fry for 5 minutes. Serve
as above.

quick beef stroganoff

Serves **4**
Preparation time **10 minutes**
Cooking time **15 minutes**

2 tablespoons **paprika**
1 tablespoon **plain flour**
450 g (14½ oz) sliced **beef
  sirloin**
300 g (10 oz) **long grain
  white rice**
25 g (1 oz) **butter**
4 tablespoons **vegetable** or
  sunflower oil
1 large **onion**, thinly sliced
250 g (8 oz) **chestnut
  mushrooms**, trimmed
  and sliced
300 ml (½ pint) **soured cream**
salt and **pepper**
1 tablespoon chopped **curly
  parsley**, to garnish

Mix together the paprika and flour in a large bowl, add the beef and turn to coat.

Cook the rice in lightly salted boiling water for 13 minutes until cooked but firm. Drain, set aside and keep warm.

Meanwhile, melt the butter and 2 tablespoons of the oil in a large frying pan and cook the onion for about 6 minutes or until soft. Add the mushrooms and cook for a further 5 minutes or until soft. Remove with a slotted spoon and set aside.

Add the remaining oil to the pan, increase the heat to high and add the beef. Fry until browned all over, then reduce the heat. Return the onion mixture to the pan along with the soured cream; bring to the boil, then reduce the heat and allow to bubble gently for 1–2 minutes. Season well.

Serve immediately with the cooked rice and a sprinkling of chopped parsley.

For mushroom & red pepper Stroganoff, omit the beef, increase the quantity of chestnut mushrooms to 500 g (1 lb) and add 2 thinly sliced red peppers. Cook the mushrooms with the onion until they have reduced and the onion is soft. Remove the mixture from the pan. Cook the peppers until tender. Return the onion mixture to the pan, as above. Sprinkle with pine nuts to serve.

pork & peppercorn tagliatelle

Serves **4**
Preparation time **10 minutes**
Cooking time **20 minutes**

350 g (11½ oz) dried
  tagliatelle verde or similar
2 tablespoons **olive oil**
500 g (1 lb) **pork tenderloin
  fillet**, sliced
1 **onion**, finely chopped
1 large **garlic clove**, chopped
2 tablespoons **brandy**
75 ml (3 fl oz) **white wine**
2 tablespoons **raisins** soaked
  in 50 ml (2 fl oz) warm **apple
  juice**
1 teaspoon chopped
  rosemary
1½ tablespoons **green
  peppercorns in brine**,
  drained and chopped
3 **juniper berries** (optional)
250 ml (8 fl oz) **single cream**
salt and **pepper**

Cook the pasta in lightly salted boiling water according to the instructions on the packet.

Meanwhile, heat the oil in a large frying pan and brown the pork slices for 2 minutes, turning once. Remove with a slotted spoon and set aside. Add the onion to the pan and cook for about 5 minutes before adding the garlic. Cook for a further minute until softened.

Pour in the brandy, wine, raisins and apple juice, rosemary, green peppercorns and juniper berries (if used), bring to the boil and bubble over high heat for 1–2 minutes. Reduce the heat, stir in the cream and simmer gently for 5 minutes.

Return the pork to the pan and stir for 3–5 minutes, or until cooked through and tender. Turn the heat off. Toss through the prepared pasta and serve.

For pork & sun-dried tomato tagliatelle, replace the raisins with chopped sun-dried tomatoes. There is no need to soak them in the apple juice, but don't omit it altogether: just add it at the same time as the tomatoes.

pepper-crusted loin of venison

Serves **4**

Preparation time **10 minutes**

Cooking time **up to 45 minutes**

750 g (1½ lb) **loin of venison**, cut from the haunch

75 g (3 oz) **mixed peppercorns**, crushed

2 tablespoons **juniper berries**, crushed

1 **egg white**, lightly beaten

salt and **pepper**

Make sure that the venison fits into your grill pan; if necessary, cut the loin in half to fit.

Mix together the peppercorns, juniper berries and some salt in a large, shallow dish. Dip the venison in the egg white, then roll it in the peppercorn mixture, covering it evenly all over.

Cook the venison under a preheated hot grill for 4 minutes on each of the four sides, turning it carefully so that the crust stays intact. Transfer the loin to a lightly greased roasting tin and cook in a preheated oven, 200°C (400°F), Gas Mark 6, for another 15 minutes for rare and up to 30 minutes for well done (the time will depend on the thickness of the loin of venison).

Leave the venison to rest for a few minutes, then slice it thickly and serve with green beans, redcurrant jelly and finely sliced sweet potato crisps.

For Chinese-style venison steaks with pak choi, omit the peppercorns and juniper berries and replace the loin of venison with four 175 g (6 oz) venison steaks. Make a marinade by mixing together 3 tablespoons soy sauce, 1 tablespoon each finely grated fresh root ginger, oyster sauce and rice wine, 2 crushed garlic cloves and 2 tablespoons groundnut oil. Marinate for up to an hour, then griddle for 3–4 minutes on each side. Serve with noodles and pak choi.

chorizo & smoked paprika penne

Serves **4**
Preparation time **15 minutes**
Cooking time **26 minutes**

1 tablespoon **olive oil**
200 g (7 oz) **chorizo sausage**, diced
1 **onion**, chopped
2 **garlic cloves**, chopped
1 teaspoon **hot smoked paprika**
1 tablespoon **capers**
1 teaspoon **dried oregano**
1 teaspoon finely grated **lemon rind**
pinch of **caster sugar**
150 g (5 oz) **roasted red pepper**, sliced
800 g (1 lb 10 oz) can **chopped tomatoes**
350 g (11½ oz) dried **penne**
salt and **pepper**

To serve
chilli oil (optional)
4 tablespoons grated **Parmesan cheese**

Heat the oil in a large pan and fry the chorizo for 2 minutes until golden. Add the onion and garlic and cook for about 5 minutes or until soft and golden.

Stir in the paprika and cook for a further minute, then add the capers, oregano, lemon rind, sugar, red pepper and tomatoes. Bring to the boil, then reduce the heat and simmer gently for 15 minutes.

Meanwhile, cook the penne in lightly salted boiling water according to the instructions on the packet.

Drain the pasta and stir it into the chorizo sauce. Serve immediately with a drizzle of chilli oil (if used) and the freshly grated Parmesan.

For garlic, oregano & Parmesan toasts, to serve as an accompaniment, split a ciabatta loaf in half lengthways and then cut each length in half. Mix 1 crushed garlic clove with 1 teaspoon dried oregano and 2 tablespoons olive oil. Drizzle over the ciabatta and scatter each piece with 1 teaspoon finely grated Parmesan. Place under a hot grill for 3–4 minutes until toasted and golden.

tartiflette-style pizza

Serves **4**

Preparation time **20 minutes**, plus resting

Cooking time **23–25 minutes**

290 g (9½ oz) **pizza base mix**

25 g (1 oz) **butter**

1 tablespoon **olive oil**

200 g (7 oz) **smoked bacon lardons** or **smoky bacon bits**

2 **onions**, sliced

1 **garlic clove**, chopped

200 ml (7 fl oz) **crème fraîche**

250 g (8 oz) cooked **potatoes**, thinly sliced

250 g (8 oz) **Reblochon cheese**, sliced

Make the pizza base according to the instructions on the packet. Form the dough into 4 balls and roll them out into ovals. Cover lightly with oiled clingfilm and leave in a warm place.

Melt the butter and olive oil in a large frying pan and fry the bacon for 3–4 minutes or until cooked. Add the onions and garlic and fry gently for 5–6 minutes or until soft and golden.

Spread 1 tablespoon of the crème fraîche over each pizza base. Top with slices of potato, some of the bacon and onion mixture and 2–3 slices of Reblochon. Cook in a preheated oven, 220°C (425°F), Gas Mark 7, for 15 minutes until bubbling and golden.

Serve immediately with an extra dollop of the remaining crème fraîche on top, if liked.

For artichoke heart & dolcelatte pizza, replace the potatoes with 2 x 475 g (15 oz) cans of artichoke hearts, drained and halved. Top with sliced dolcelatte.

poultry

lime, ginger & coriander chicken

Serves **4**

Preparation time
5–10 minutes

Cooking time **50 minutes**

3 **limes**

1 cm (½ inch) cube **fresh root ginger**, peeled and finely grated

4 tablespoons finely chopped **coriander**, plus extra leaves to serve

2 teaspoons **vegetable oil**

4 **chicken legs**

300 g (10 oz) **Thai jasmine rice**

salt

Finely grate the rind of 2 of the limes and halve these limes. Mix the rind with the ginger and coriander in a non-metallic bowl and stir in 1 teaspoon of the oil to make a rough paste.

Carefully lift the skin from the chicken legs and push under the ginger paste. Pull the skin back into place, then cut 3–4 slashes in the thickest parts of the legs and brush with the remaining oil.

Put the legs in a roasting tin, flesh-side down, with the halved limes and cook in a preheated oven, 220°C (425°F), Gas Mark 7, for 45–50 minutes, basting occasionally. The legs are cooked when the meat comes away from the bone and the juices run clear.

Meanwhile, put the rice in a pan with 400 ml (14 fl oz) cold water, cover with a tight-fitting lid and cook over a medium-low heat for 10 minutes until the water has been absorbed and the rice is almost cooked. Set aside somewhere warm until the chicken has finished cooking.

Spoon the rice into small bowls to mould, then turn it on to serving plates. Add the chicken legs, squeeze over the roasted lime and scatter with coriander leaves. Serve immediately with the remaining lime, cut into wedges.

For Mediterranean chicken, replace the ginger paste with a red pesto made by blending 6 sun-dried tomatoes, 1 tablespoon pine nuts, ½ clove chopped garlic, 1 tablespoon chopped basil, 1 teaspoon grated lemon rind, 1 tablespoon lemon juice, 3 tablespoons olive oil and 1 tablespoon grated Parmesan cheese.

asian steamed-chicken salad

Serves **4**

Preparation time **10 minutes, plus cooling**

Cooking time **8–10 minutes**

4 boneless, skinless **chicken breasts**, about 150 g (5 oz) each

½ small **Chinese cabbage**, finely shredded

1 large **carrot**, grated

200 g (7 oz) **bean sprouts**

small bunch of **coriander**, finely chopped

small bunch of **mint**, finely chopped

1 **red chilli**, deseeded and finely sliced (optional)

Dressing

125 ml (4 fl oz) **sunflower oil**

juice of 2 **limes**

1½ tablespoons **Thai fish sauce**

3 tablespoons **light soy sauce**

1 tablespoon finely chopped fresh **root ginger**

Put the chicken breasts in a bamboo or other steamer set over a large pan of simmering water. Cover and leave to steam for about 8 minutes or until the chicken is cooked through. Alternatively, poach the chicken for 8–10 minutes until the meat is cooked and tender.

Meanwhile, make the dressing by mixing together the ingredients in a bowl.

When the chicken is cool enough to handle, cut or tear it into strips and mix the pieces with 2 tablespoons of the dressing. Leave to cool.

Toss all the vegetables and herbs together and arrange in serving dishes. Scatter over the cold chicken and serve immediately with the remaining dressing.

For Asian steamed-prawn salad with peanuts, use 450 g (14½ oz) medium-sized raw, peeled prawns steamed in the same way as the chicken for 2–3 minutes until pink and firm. Finish with a couple of tablespoons of crushed unsalted peanuts.

chicken with spring vegetables

Serves **4**

Preparation time **10 minutes**, plus resting

Cooking time **about 1¼ hours**

1.5 kg (3 lb) **chicken**

about 1.5 litres (2½ pints) hot **chicken stock**

2 **shallots**, halved

2 **garlic cloves**

2 sprigs of **parsley**

2 sprigs of **marjoram**

2 sprigs of **lemon thyme**

2 **carrots**, halved

1 **leek**, trimmed and sliced

200 g (7 oz) **tenderstem broccoli**

250 g (8 oz) **asparagus**, trimmed

½ **Savoy cabbage**, shredded

Put the chicken in a large saucepan and pour over enough stock just to cover the chicken. Push the shallots, garlic, herbs, carrots and leek into the pan and place over a medium-high heat. Bring to the boil, then reduce the heat and simmer gently for 1 hour or until the chicken is falling away from the bones.

Add the remaining vegetables to the pan and simmer for a further 6–8 minutes or until the vegetables are cooked.

Turn off the heat and leave to rest for 5–10 minutes before serving the chicken and vegetables in deep bowls with spoonfuls of the broth. Remove the skin, if preferred, and serve with plenty of crusty bread.

For Chinese chicken soup, use the same amount of stock and but omit all the vegetables and herbs. Instead, use a sliced 8 cm (3 inch) length of fresh root ginger, 2 garlic cloves, sliced, 1 teaspoon Chinese five spice powder, 4–5 whole star anise and 100 ml (3½ fl oz) dark soy sauce. Add baby corn and mangetout instead of the spring vegetables and cook as above.

lemon chilli chicken

Serves **4**

Preparation time **25 minutes**,
   plus marinating

Cooking time **45 minutes**

1.75 kg (3½ lb) **chicken**, cut
   into 8 pieces

8 **garlic cloves**

4 juicy **lemons**, squeezed,
   skins reserved

1 small **red chilli**, deseeded
   and chopped

2 tablespoons **orange flower
   honey**

4 tablespoons chopped
   parsley, plus sprigs
   to garnish

salt and **pepper**

Arrange the chicken pieces in a shallow flameproof dish. Peel and crush 2 of the garlic cloves and add them to the lemon juice with the chilli and honey. Stir well, then pour this mixture over the chicken. Tuck the lemon skins around the meat, cover and leave to marinate in the refrigerator for at least 2 hours or overnight, turning once or twice.

Turn the chicken pieces so they are skin side up, scatter over the remaining whole garlic cloves and put the lemon skins, cut sides down, on top.

Cook the chicken in a preheated oven, 200°C (400°F), Gas Mark 6, for 45 minutes or until golden brown and tender. Stir in the parsley, season to taste and serve garnished with parsley sprigs.

For coriander rice & peas to serve as an accompaniment, boil 250 g (8 oz) frozen peas for about 3 minutes, drain them and toss them in 50 g (2 oz) melted butter with 2 chopped spring onions and a handful of chopped fresh coriander. Fork the peas into the rice and serve.

chicken with spiced rice

Serves **4**
Preparation time **5 minutes**
Cooking time **30–35 minutes**

4 boneless, skinless **chicken
   breasts**, about 150 g (5 oz)
   each
4 tablespoons **olive oil**
1 **onion**, finely chopped
2 **garlic cloves**, crushed
2 teaspoons **ground
   cinnamon**
1 teaspoon **ground allspice**
¼ teaspoon **cayenne pepper**
1 teaspoon **salt**
¼ teaspoon **ground cloves**
½ teaspoon **ground nutmeg**
½ teaspoon **ground ginger**
½ teaspoon **black pepper**
300 g (10 oz) **long grain rice**
750 ml (1¼ pint) hot **chicken
   stock**
2 tablespoons finely chopped
   parsley, to garnish

Brush the chicken breasts with 1 tablespoon of the
oil and cook under a preheated hot grill or in a griddle
pan for about 1 minute on each side until golden
brown but not cooked through. Set aside.

Heat the remaining oil in a large, heavy-based pan or
casserole over a medium heat and cook the onion for
5–6 minutes or until softened. Stir in the garlic and
cook for 1 minute, then add the spices and seasoning.
Continue cooking, stirring frequently, for a further
2 minutes.

Add the rice to the spice mixture, stirring well so that
each grain is coated, then pour in the stock and return
the chicken to the pan. Bring to the boil and cover
with a tight-fitting lid, then reduce the heat and leave
to simmer gently over a medium-low heat for about
15–20 minutes until the chicken and rice are cooked.

Sprinkle with parsley and serve.

For spiced-rice stuffed roast chicken, prepare
the rice as above, cooking for a total of 10 minutes.
Drain, reserving the stock. Use the rice to stuff a
1.5 kg (3 lb) roasting chicken. Place the chicken in a
casserole dish, season, then pour the stock into the
dish and add 150 ml (¼ pint) white wine. Cover and
roast at 190°C (375°F), Gas Mark 5 for 1¼ hours.
Uncover, baste with the pan juices and roast for a
further 30 minutes.

chicken alla milanese

Serves **4**

Preparation time **12 minutes**

Cooking time **20 minutes**

1 kg (2 lb) **floury potatoes**, peeled and cut in half

4 boneless, skinless **chicken breasts**, about 150 g (5 oz) each

2 small **eggs**, beaten

3 tablespoons **olive oil**

150 g (5 oz) **butter**

4 ripe **tomatoes**, roughly chopped

2 tablespoons **capers in brine**, drained and rinsed

4 tablespoons **white wine**

4 tablespoons **lemon juice**

100 g (3½ oz) **rocket**

salt and **pepper**

Crust

2 teaspoons **dried oregano**

100 g (3½ oz) **breadcrumbs**

½ teaspoon **garlic powder**

finely grated rind of 1 **lemon**

50 g (2 oz) **Parmesan cheese**, finely grated

Cook the potatoes in lightly salted boiling water for about 20 minutes or until soft.

Meanwhile, mix together the ingredients for the crust and tip the mixture on to a plate. Put the chicken breasts between 2 sheets of clingfilm or greaseproof paper and batter with a rolling pin or mallet until flat. Dip the chicken into the beaten egg, then press into the crust mixture to coat.

Heat the oil in a large frying pan and cook the chicken for 3 minutes on each side or until cooked through and golden. Set aside and keep warm.

Add half the butter to the pan and stir in the tomatoes, capers and white wine. Season and allow to bubble for 2–3 minutes.

Drain and mash the potatoes with the lemon juice, the remaining butter and plenty of seasoning. Spoon on to serving plates with the crispy chicken. Quickly stir the rocket into the tomatoes and pile a little on to each piece of chicken. Serve immediately.

For spinach with raisins & pine nuts to serve as an accompaniment, put 1 chopped onion, 4 tablespoons raisins and 50 g (2 oz) butter in a large pan. Add 1 kg (2 lb) spinach and 3 tablespoons water. Cover and cook for 3–5 minutes, shaking the pan occasionally, until the spinach has wilted. Mix well and serve.

honey-spiced chicken breasts

Serves **4**
Preparation time **8 minutes**
Cooking time **20–25 minutes**

4 boneless **chicken breasts**,
  with skins, about 150 g
  (5 oz) each

Spiced honey
2 tablespoons **mango
  chutney**
1 tablespoon **clear honey**
2 teaspoons **Worcestershire
  sauce**
1 teaspoon **garlic powder**
1 teaspoon **piri piri sauce**
2 tablespoons **red wine
  vinegar**
2 teaspoons **wholegrain
  mustard**
salt and **pepper**

Slash the chicken breasts 3–4 times with a sharp knife, then place in a baking dish.

Mix together all the ingredients for the spiced honey and spoon over the chicken. Toss until well coated.

Put the chicken in a preheated oven, 220°C (425°F), Gas Mark 7, for 20–25 minutes or until the meat is cooked through and the skin is crispy.

Leave the chicken to rest for a few minutes before serving with chunky potato chips, if liked.

For herbed honey chicken with sweet potato chips, replace the spiced honey with a herbed honey sauce, as follows. Mix 2 tablespoons of honey and 2 tablespoons cider vinegar with 1 tablespoon each of chopped thyme, tarragon and sage. Spoon over the chicken, as above, and serve with chunky sweet potato chips, if liked.

crispy duck with ginger & orange

Serves **4**
Preparation time **10 minutes**
Cooking time **24–26 minutes**

1 teaspoon **vegetable oil**
4 **duck breasts**, skin slashed
350 g (11½ oz) **spring greens**, shredded
1 tablespoon **balsamic vinegar**
1 piece **conserved ginger in syrup,** chopped
50 ml (2 fl oz) strong **orange and cinnamon tea** infusion (or other citrus tea)
½ teaspoon **mixed peppercorns**, crushed
salt

Heat the oil in a frying pan over a medium heat and fry the duck breasts, skin-side down, for about 15 minutes until the skin is really crispy. Drain off the excess fat, turn the duck over and fry for a further 5 minutes. Remove and keep warm.

Put the spring greens in a steamer over a pan of boiling water and steam for 2–3 minutes or until wilted.

Add the remaining ingredients to the frying pan and season with salt to taste, then stir to mix and allow to bubble for 2–3 minutes.

Serve the duck breasts with the sauce poured over and with the steamed spring greens.

For duck with sherry-lime marmalade, omit the vinegar, ginger and tea and instead make a sauce with 4 tablespoons dry sherry and 4 tablespoons lime marmalade. Sprinkle a handful of chopped mint on to the spring greens before serving.

thai chicken shells with coriander

Serves **4**
Preparation time **10 minutes**
Cooking time **15 minutes**

1 teaspoon **vegetable oil**
2 **chicken breasts**, about
    150 g (5 oz) each, sliced
1 tablespoon red or green
    Thai curry paste
400 ml (14 fl oz) can **coconut
    milk**
250 g (8 oz) **basmati rice**
3 tablespoons chopped fresh
    coriander
3 **spring onions**, sliced
4 **Little Gem lettuces**,
    separated into individual
    leaves
2 **limes**, cut into wedges

Heat the oil in a nonstick frying pan, add the chicken and fry for 2 minutes.

Add the curry paste and continue to fry for 1 minute, then add half the coconut milk, bring to the boil and simmer gently for 10 minutes.

Meanwhile, put the rice in a saucepan with the remaining coconut milk and 100 ml (3½ fl oz) water. Bring to the boil, then reduce the heat, cover and simmer for 10–12 minutes until the liquid is absorbed, adding a little extra water if necessary. Turn the heat off and stir in the coriander.

Put chicken and spring onion slices and some rice on a lettuce leaf and squeeze the lime wedges over the filled shells before eating.

For quick Chinese-style stir-fry, cook 300 g (10 oz) chicken strips for 1 minute in 50 ml (2 fl oz) vegetable oil with 1 tablespoon chopped garlic. Add 150 g (5 oz) sliced green pepper and 5 deseeded and sliced red chillies and cook for a minute, then stir in 75 g (3 oz) sliced onion, 1 tablespoon oyster sauce, 1 teaspoon fish sauce, ½ tablespoon light soy sauce and ¼ teaspoon dark soy sauce. Stir-fry until the chicken is cooked through then serve.

smoked duck salad

Serves **4**

Preparation time **15 minutes**

150 g (5 oz) **lamb's lettuce**
1½ **oranges** or **blood
 oranges**, cut into segments
100 g (3½ oz) **smoked duck
 breast**, thinly sliced
seeds of 1 **pomegranate**
50 g (2 oz) **shelled
 pistachios**

Dressing

juice of ½ **blood orange**
1 small **shallot**, finely chopped
1 tablespoon **red wine
 vinegar**
1 teaspoon **wholegrain
 mustard**
4 tablespoons **olive oil**

Arrange the lamb's lettuce on 4 large serving plates, add the orange segments and slices of duck. Scatter over the pomegranate seeds and pistachios.

Make the dressing by putting the ingredients in a screw-top jar and shaking well to combine. Drizzle the dressing over each salad, and serve immediately.

For duck & watercress salad with cranberries & pecans, replace the lamb's lettuce with watercress and the pomegranate seeds and pistachios with 4 tablespoons dried cranberries and 50 g (2 oz) chopped pecans.

baked turkey burrito

Serves **4**
Preparation time **12 minutes**
Cooking time **30–33 minutes**

4 tablespoons **vegetable oil**
500 g (1 lb) **turkey breast**,
　thinly sliced
1 large **onion**, sliced
1 **red pepper**, cored,
　deseeded and sliced
1 **yellow pepper**, cored,
　deseeded and sliced
150 g (5 oz) can **red kidney
　beans**, rinsed and drained
150 g (5 oz) **cooked rice**
juice of 1 **lime**
8 medium-sized **plain flour
　tortillas**
6 tablespoons medium-hot
　ready-made **salsa**
2 tablespoons sliced,
　**preserved jalapeño
　peppers** (optional)
250 g (8 oz) **Cheddar
　cheese**, grated
salt and **pepper**

To serve
guacamole
½ **iceberg lettuce**, shredded

Heat 2 tablespoons of the oil in a large frying pan and stir-fry the sliced turkey for 3–4 minutes until it is beginning to colour, then remove it with a slotted spoon. Increase the heat, add the remaining oil and fry the onion and peppers for 5–6 minutes, stirring only occasionally so that they colour quickly without softening too much.

Reduce the heat, return the turkey to the pan and stir in the beans and cooked rice. Season well, squeeze over the lime juice and remove from the heat. Spoon the filling on to the tortillas, roll them up and arrange them in a rectangular ovenproof dish.

Pour the salsa over the tortillas and scatter over the jalapeño peppers (if used) and Cheddar. Cook in a preheated oven, 200°C (400°F), Gas Mark 6, for about 20 minutes, until hot and the cheese has melted. Serve immediately with guacamole and shredded lettuce.

For hot tomato salsa to serve as an accompaniment, chop 500 g (1 lb) tomatoes, 1 hot red chilli, 1 garlic clove and 1 small onion. Add 2 tablespoons tomato purée, 2 tablespoons red wine vinegar and 2 tablespoons sugar. Mix well. Alternatively, blend all the ingredients in a food processor until finely chopped.

roast poussins with oregano

Serves **4**

Preparation time **10 minutes**, plus resting

Cooking time **55 minutes**

50 g (2 oz) **butter**

finely grated rind of 1 **lemon**

2 tablespoons **oregano**, chopped

1 large **garlic clove**, crushed

2 **poussins**, about 500 g (1 lb) each

150 g (5 oz) **peppery mixed salad leaves**

salt and **pepper**

Mash together the butter, lemon rind, oregano, garlic and seasoning. Lift the skin from the poussins and slide the flavoured butter between the flesh and skin, or, if you prefer, smear the butter over the skin.

Put the poussins side by side in a roasting tin and cook in a preheated oven, 220°C (425°F), Gas Mark 7, for about 55 minutes, basting occasionally, until golden and crispy and the juices run clear. Remove from the oven and leave to rest for 5 minutes.

Transfer the poussins to a chopping board and use a long, sharp knife to cut each one carefully in half lengthways. Serve immediately with the salad leaves.

For classic potato gratin, to serve as an accompaniment and which can be cooked in the oven at the same time as the poussins, use 750 g (1½ lb) peeled and thinly sliced potatoes, blanched for a minute or two in boiling, salted water. Drain the potatoes and tip them into a large, oven-proof dish. Scatter over 2 finely chopped garlic cloves and season. Pour over 350 ml (12 fl oz) double cream and sprinkle with a little grated nutmeg. Dot with 50 g (2 oz) butter, then put the dish in the oven for around 45 minutes or until soft when pieced with a knife.

hot duck & coconut noodles

Serves **4**
Preparation time **10 minutes**
Cooking time **15 minutes**

4 **confit duck legs**
250 ml (8 fl oz) **coconut milk**
200 ml (7 fl oz) **chicken stock**
2 tablespoons **Thai fish sauce**
3 whole **star anise**
1 teaspoon **chilli flakes**
25 g (1 oz) **fresh root ginger**, thinly sliced
1 small bunch of **coriander**, chopped
juice of 2 **limes**
250 g (8 oz) **flat rice noodles**
4 tablespoons **coconut shavings**, toasted
50 g (2 oz) **cashew nuts**, toasted

Heat a large frying pan and put the duck legs and their fat, skin-side down, in the pan. Cook over a medium heat for 10 minutes until the skins turn golden and crispy. Turn and cook for a further 2–3 minutes until the legs are heated through. Drain on kitchen paper, then tear the meat into small pieces and discard the bones.

Meanwhile, pour the coconut milk into a pan with the stock, fish sauce, star anise, chilli flakes, ginger and half the chopped coriander and bring to simmering point. Leave to bubble gently for 10 minutes to allow the flavours to infuse. Stir in the lime juice.

Cook the noodles in unsalted boiling water for about 3 minutes or according to the instructions on the packet, then drain and heap into serving bowls.

Scatter over the duck meat and pour over the hot coconut broth. Sprinkle with the coconut shavings, cashews and remaining coriander. Serve immediately.

For spiced prawn stir-fry, omit the duck and instead mix 400 g (13 oz) raw prawns with 25 g (1 oz) freshly grated ginger, 1 crushed garlic clove, 1 freshly chopped red chilli and 1 tablespoon vegetable oil. Heat a wok until smoking, add another tablespoon vegetable oil and stir-fry the prawns for 2–3 minutes until pink and cooked through. Serve with the noodles and a ladle of the hot coconut broth, finishing as before with cashews and coriander.

chicken with spinach chermoula

Serves **4**
Preparation time **12 minutes**
Cooking time **25 minutes**

4 boneless, skinless **chicken
  breasts**, about 175 g (6 oz)
  each, cut into large pieces
2 tablespoons **olive oil**
1 large **red onion**, sliced
400 g (13 oz) can **chickpeas**,
  rinsed and drained
8 ready-to-eat **dried apricots**,
  sliced
pinch of **saffron**
200 g (7 oz) **spinach leaves**,
  stalks removed
½ small **preserved lemon**,
  finely diced (optional)
small bunch of **coriander**,
  roughly chopped
small bunch of **flat leaf
  parsley**, roughly chopped

Chermoula
3 tablespoons ready-made
  chermoula mix
1 teaspoon **harissa paste**
juice of 1 **lemon**
100 ml (3½ fl oz) **olive oil**

Make the chermoula by putting all the ingredients in
a screw-top jar and shaking to combine. Mix half the
paste with the chicken and set aside.

Heat the oil in a large frying pan over a medium heat
and fry the onion for about 8 minutes until soft and
golden. Increase the heat a little, tip in the coated
chicken and cook for about 12 minutes, stirring
frequently. Stir in the chickpeas, apricots, saffron and
the remaining chermoula paste and cook for a further
3–4 minutes. The chicken and spices should be
cooked through.

Stir in the spinach and cook until just wilted, then add
the preserved lemon (if used) and herbs. Serve
immediately on warm pitta or flat breads.

For homemade chermoula, instead of the ready-
made chermoula mix, stir together 2 teaspoons
ground cumin, 2 teaspoons ground coriander,
1 teaspoon turmeric, 1 teaspoon salt and 1 teaspoon
ground black pepper.

turkey & pumpkin seed salad

Serves **4**
Preparation time **12 minutes**
Cooking time **6 minutes**

3 tablespoons **sunflower oil**
400 g (13 oz) minced **turkey**
1 tablespoon **preserved jalapeño peppers**, sliced
200 g (7 oz) can **sweetcorn**, drained
1 ripe **avocado**, peeled, stoned and cut into chunks
2 ripe **tomatoes**, chopped
1 small **red onion**, finely diced
small bunch of **coriander**, chopped
salt and **pepper**

Dressing
juice of 2 **limes**
1 teaspoon **clear honey**
4 tablespoons **pumpkin seed oil**

To serve
½ small **red cabbage**, shredded
250 g (8 oz) **buffalo mozzarella cheese**, cubed
4 **taco shells**
3 tablespoons **pumpkin seeds**, to sprinkle

Make the dressing by mixing together the ingredients in a small bowl. Season to taste and set aside.

Heat the oil in a large frying pan and fry the turkey for 5–6 minutes until cooked and beginning to colour. Scrape into a bowl, mix with half the dressing and set aside to cool.

Make a chunky salsa by combining the peppers, sweetcorn, avocado, tomatoes, red onion and coriander. Mix with the remaining dressing.

When the turkey is cool, mix it with the salsa and serve with the cabbage, mozzarella and taco shells with the pumpkin seeds scattered over.

For turkey with white cabbage & sunflower seed salad, replace the pumpkin-seed oil in the dressing with olive oil and the red cabbage with white cabbage. Substitute the mozzarella with finely diced Gruyére or Gouda and the pumpkin seeds with sunflower seeds. Omit the tacos, serving the salad as a base with the turkey mix on top.

84

turkey & wild mushroom pasties

Serves **4**
Preparation time **8 minutes**,
  plus soaking
Cooking time **29–32 minutes**

25 g (1 oz) **dried wild
  mushrooms**
4 tablespoons **olive oil**
450 g (14½ oz) **turkey breast**,
  sliced
100 g (3½ oz) **prosciutto**, torn
  into pieces
200 g (7 oz) **field** or
  portabello mushrooms,
  trimmed and sliced
100 ml (3½ fl oz) **red wine**
1 teaspoon chopped **thyme**
250 g (8 oz) **mascarpone
  cheese**
500 g (1 lb) **puff pastry**
  (thawed if frozen)
1 **egg**, beaten
salt and **pepper**
watercress, to garnish

Soak the mushrooms in 4 tablespoons boiling water
for 5–10 minutes. Heat 2 tablespoons of the oil in a
frying pan and fry the turkey for 2–3 minutes until
golden. Add the prosciutto and cook for 2 minutes
before adding the fresh and dried mushrooms. Fry for
3–4 minutes until the mushrooms are soft and golden.

Pour the wine into the pan, then add the thyme. Allow
the liquid to bubble for 2–3 minutes until evaporated.
Remove from the heat, stir in the mascarpone and
season to taste.

Roll out the pastry into a rectangular shape until it
forms a thin layer and cut into four. Spoon one-quarter
of the mixture on to the centre of each quarter of
pastry. Brush a little beaten egg around the edges, fold
over the pastry and press firmly to seal.

Brush the remaining egg over the closed pasties,
score the tops with a knife, if liked, and cook in a
preheated oven, 200°C (400°F), Gas Mark 6, for
20 minutes until golden and crispy.

For turkey & mushroom pie, increase the wine
to 300 ml (½ pint) and simmer for 5 minutes. Finish
the filling as above. Replace the puff pastry with
shortcrust. Roll it out into a thick layer to cover a
22 cm (9 inch) pie dish with an overlap of 5 cm
(2 inches). Cut a strip of pastry 1 cm (½ inch) wide
and put it round the rim of the dish. Add the filling and
cover with the remaining pastry. Glaze with egg and
bake in a preheated oven, 200°C (400°F), Gas Mark
6, for 20 minutes then lower the heat to 180°C
(350°F), Gas Mark 4 for a further 10–15 minutes.

spicy basque-style chicken

Serves **4**
Preparation time **12 minutes**
Cooking time **45–47 minutes**

1 kg (2 lb) **chicken pieces**
   (thighs, drumsticks, etc.)
1 heaped tablespoon
   seasoned flour
3 tablespoons **olive oil**
1 **onion**, sliced
1 **red pepper**, cored,
   deseeded and sliced
1 **green pepper**, cored,
   deseeded and sliced
2 **garlic cloves**, crushed
1 teaspoon **paprika**
1 teaspoon **hot smoked**
   paprika
100 g (3½ oz) **prosciutto**,
   torn into pieces
75 ml (3 fl oz) **Marsala**
150 ml (¼ pint) **white wine**
400 g (13 oz) can **chopped**
   tomatoes
1 teaspoon **dried thyme**
salt and **pepper**

Dust the chicken in the seasoned flour. Heat the oil in a large, heavy-based casserole over a medium-high heat and fry the chicken until golden brown. Remove and set aside.

Reduce the heat, add the onion and peppers and cook, stirring frequently, for 4–5 minutes until softened and golden. Stir in the garlic, paprikas and prosciutto and fry for a further 1–2 minutes.

Return the chicken to the pan, pour in the Marsala, wine, 100 ml (3½ fl oz) water and the tomatoes. Stir in the thyme and season to taste. Bring to the boil, then reduce the heat to a simmer, cover the pan and leave for 30–35 minutes until the chicken is cooked and the sauce is rich and thick.

Serve the chicken in bowls with lots of sauce.

For pan-fried polenta with olives to serve as an accompaniment, cut 2 x 500 g (1 lb) packets of ready-made polenta into 2.5 cm (1 inch) slices. Fry the slices in olive oil and sprinkle with 2 tablespoons chopped black olives and 1 teaspoon chopped fresh parsley. Add 1 crushed garlic clove and fry quickly. Serve as above.

fish

pan-fried haddock fillets

Serves **4**
Preparation time **15 minutes**
Cooking time **20 minutes**

1 kg (2 lb) **floury potatoes**,
   peeled
75 ml (3 fl oz) **full-fat milk**
150 g (5 oz) **butter**
4 **haddock fillets**, about
   150 g (5 oz) each, skin on
2 tablespoons **capers in
   brine**, drained and rinsed
4 tablespoons **lemon juice**
salt and **pepper**

Cook the potatoes in lightly salted boiling water for about 20 minutes. Mash until smooth with the milk and 50 g (2 oz) of the butter. Season well.

Meanwhile, melt the remaining butter in a large frying pan, add the haddock fillets, skin-side down, and cook for about 3 minutes until golden and crispy. Carefully turn over the fillets and cook for a further 1–2 minutes.

Remove the fillets and transfer to serving plates with the mashed potato.

Return the pan to the hob. Increase the heat until the butter turns nut-brown in colour, then add the capers and lemon juice. Bubble for a minute and then spoon over the fish and potatoes. Serve immediately.

For trout fillets with almonds, replace the haddock fillets with trout fillets and fry as above, finishing with almonds instead of capers.

king prawns with japanese salad

Serves **4**

Preparation time **10 minutes, plus cooling**

Cooking time **3 minutes**

400 g (13 oz) **raw, peeled king prawns**

200 g (7 oz) **bean sprouts**

125 g (4 oz) **mangetout**, shredded

100 g (3½ oz) **water chestnuts**, thinly sliced

½ **iceberg lettuce**, shredded

12 **radishes**, thinly sliced

1 tablespoon **sesame seeds**, lightly toasted

Dressing

2 tablespoons **rice vinegar**

125 ml (4 fl oz) **sunflower oil**

1 teaspoon **five spice powder** (optional)

2 tablespoons **mirin**

Set a steamer over a pan of simmering water and steam the king prawns for 2–3 minutes until cooked and pink. Set aside and leave to cool.

Make the dressing by mixing together all the ingredients in a small bowl.

Toss together the bean sprouts, mangetout, water chestnuts, lettuce and radishes and scatter over the prawns and sesame seeds. Drizzle over the dressing and serve immediately.

For chilli sauce to serve as an accompaniment, combine 1 finely chopped garlic clove, ½ teaspoon finely grated fresh root ginger, 2 teaspoons light soy sauce, 1 tablespoon sweet chilli sauce and ½ tablespoon tomato ketchup. Mix well.

butter bean & anchovy pâté

Serves **2–3**
Preparation time **5 minutes**

425 g (14 oz) can **butter
  beans**, drained and rinsed
50 g (2 oz) can **anchovy
  fillets** in oil
2 **spring onions**, finely
  chopped
2 tablespoons **lemon juice**
1 tablespoon **olive oil**
4 tablespoons chopped
  coriander
salt and **pepper**

To serve
lemon wedges
4–6 slices **rye bread**, toasted

Put all the ingredients except the coriander in a food
processor or blender and process until well mixed but
not smooth. Alternatively, mash the beans with a fork,
finely chop the anchovies and mix the ingredients
together by hand.

Stir in the coriander and season well. Serve with lemon
wedges and accompanied with toasted rye bread.

For butter bean & mushroom pâté, replace the
anchovies with 250 g (8 oz) sliced mushrooms. Cook
these in 2 tablespoons olive oil with 1 finely chopped
garlic clove until greatly reduced and all juices have
evaporated. Cool. Purée the mushrooms in a food
processor or blender, or mash with a fork, and add the
butter beans, processing or mixing as above.

quick tuna steak with green salsa

Serves **4**

Preparation time **14 minutes**,
  plus marinating

Cooking time **2–4 minutes**

2 tablespoons **olive oil**

grated rind of 1 **lemon**

2 teaspoons chopped **parsley**

½ teaspoon crushed **coriander
  seeds**

4 fresh **tuna steaks**, about
  150 g (5 oz) each

salt and **pepper**

dressed **lettuce salad**,
  to serve

Salsa

2 tablespoons **capers**,
  chopped

2 tablespoons chopped
  cornichons

1 tablespoon finely chopped
  parsley

2 teaspoons chopped **chives**

2 teaspoons finely chopped
  chervil

30 g (1½ oz) pitted **green
  olives**, chopped

1 **shallot**, finely chopped
  (optional)

2 tablespoons **lemon juice**

2 tablespoons **olive oil**

Mix together the oil, lemon rind, parsley and coriander seeds with plenty of pepper in a bowl. Rub the tuna steaks with the mixture.

Combine the ingredients for the salsa, season to taste and set aside.

Heat a griddle or frying pan until hot and cook the tuna steaks for 1–2 minutes on each side to cook partially. The tuna should be well seared but rare. Remove and allow to rest for a couple of minutes.

Serve the tuna steaks with a spoonful of salsa, a dressed salad and plenty of fresh crusty bread.

For yellow pepper & mustard salsa, combine the following: 2 yellow peppers, finely chopped; 1 tablespoon Dijon mustard; 2 tablespoons each finely chopped chives, parsley and dill; 1 teaspoon sugar; 1 tablespoon cider vinegar and 2 tablespoons olive oil.

scallops with pancetta

Serves **4**
Preparation time **10 minutes**,
plus cooling time
Cooking time **15 minutes**

8 small vine-ripened
tomatoes, halved
2 **garlic cloves**, finely
chopped
8 **basil leaves**
2 tablespoons **olive oil**
2 tablespoons **balsamic
vinegar**
8 thin slices of **pancetta**
16–20 **king scallops**, corals
and muscles removed
8 canned **artichoke hearts in
oil**, drained and halved
125 g (4 oz) **lamb's lettuce**,
trimmed
salt and **pepper**

Arrange the tomatoes close together, cut side up, in a roasting tin. Scatter over the chopped garlic and basil, drizzle with 1 tablespoon each of the oil and balsamic vinegar and season well with salt and pepper. Cook in a preheated oven, 220°C (425°F), Gas Mark 7, for 15 minutes.

Meanwhile, cook the pancetta slices in a preheated hot griddle pan for about 2 minutes, turning once, until crisp and golden. Transfer to a plate lined with kitchen paper until needed.

Quickly sear the scallops for 1 minute in the hot griddle, then turn them over and cook for a further minute on the other side until cooked and starting to caramelize. Remove, cover with foil and leave to rest for 2 minutes.

Meanwhile, cook the artichoke hearts for about 2 minutes until hot and charred.

Toss the lamb's lettuce with the remaining oil and balsamic vinegar and arrange on serving plates. Top with the artichokes, tomatoes, crispy pancetta and scallops. Serve immediately.

For salmon & pancetta salad, omit the tomatoes and cook the pancetta, as above. Instead of the scallops, use a chunky 450 g (14½oz) fresh salmon fillet. Brush the salmon lightly with olive oil before searing on a hot griddle for 2–3 minutes until golden, turning once. Cook the artichoke hearts as above. Substitute the lamb's lettuce with rocket and shredded Little Gem hearts. Toss and arrange as above.

prawns with sesame noodles

Serves **4**
Preparation time **8 minutes**
Cooking time **6 minutes**

250 g (8 oz) **egg noodles**
1 tablespoon **sesame oil**, plus
   extra to serve
1 tablespoon **vegetable oil**
1 **yellow pepper**, cored,
   deseeded and sliced
1 **red pepper**, cored,
   deseeded and sliced
75 g (3 oz) **shiitake** or
   chestnut mushrooms,
   trimmed and thinly sliced
1 large **carrot**, peeled and cut
   into thin sticks
2 **spring onions**, thinly sliced
   lengthways
1 **red chilli**, finely chopped
300 g (10 oz) **large cooked
   peeled prawns**
1 tablespoon **sesame seeds**,
   lightly toasted

Cook the noodles in a large saucepan of unsalted water for 4 minutes or according to the instructions on the packet.

Meanwhile, heat a large wok over a high heat until smoking. Add the oils and stir-fry the peppers for 1–2 minutes. Add the mushrooms, cook for 1 minute, then add the carrot and cook for a further minute. Add the spring onions, chilli and prawns and stir-fry for 2 minutes.

Drain the noodles and add them to the wok. Mix to combine, heat through, then scatter with the sesame seeds and serve immediately.

For teriyaki prawns with vegetables on soba,
substitute the egg noodles for soba noodles (made with buckwheat flour). Prepare the vegetables and noodles as above but cook the prawns separately, adding 1 sliced garlic clove and 4 tablespoons ready-made teriyaki sauce. Serve the prawns on the soba noodles and sprinkle with coriander instead of sesame seeds.

crunchy swordfish with puy lentils

Serves **4**
Preparation time **12 minutes**
Cooking time **15 minutes**

4 skinless **swordfish fillets**,
   about 175 g (6 oz) each
2 tablespoons **olive oil**
500 g (1 lb) cooked **Puy
   lentils**, heated
8 **sun-blushed tomatoes**,
   roughly chopped
small bunch of **basil**, shredded
1 tablespoon **capers in brine**,
   drained and rinsed
4 **spring onions**, finely sliced
8 pitted **black olives**, roughly
   chopped
2 tablespoons **olive oil**
salt and **pepper**
2 **lemons**, halved, to serve

Crust
75 g (3 oz) **breadcrumbs**
grated rind of 1 **lemon**
1 teaspoon finely chopped
   rosemary
2 tablespoons finely chopped
   parsley

Mix together the ingredients for the crust and add
some salt and pepper. Rub the fish fillets in the oil
and then press them into the crust mixture to coat.

Transfer the fish to a nonstick baking sheet and
carefully tip over the remaining crust. Cook in a
preheated oven, 220°C (425°F), Gas Mark 7, for
15 minutes until the fish is flaky and the crust is
golden and crunchy.

Put the hot lentils in a bowl and stir in the remaining
ingredients. Serve immediately with the fish fillets and
lemon halves.

For crunchy hake with Mediterranean potatoes,
replace the swordfish with 4 x 200 g (7 oz) hake
steaks and prepare as above. Instead of the lentils,
peel and halve 700 g (1 lb 7 oz) red new potatoes,
boil them for 10–15 minutes, drain, then toss with the
other ingredients.

blackened cod with citrus salsa

Serves **4**
Preparation time **15 minutes**
Cooking time **15 minutes**

1 large **orange**
1 **garlic clove**, crushed
2 large **tomatoes**, deseeded
  and diced
2 tablespoons chopped **basil**,
  plus extra to garnish
75 g (3 oz) pitted **black
  olives**, chopped
5 tablespoons **olive oil**
4 **cod fillets**, about 175 g
  (6 oz) each
1 tablespoon **jerk seasoning**
salt and **pepper**

Cut the skin and the white membrane off the orange. Working over a bowl to catch the juice, cut between the membranes to remove the segments. Halve the segments and mix them with the reserved juice and the garlic, tomatoes, basil, olives and 4 tablespoons of the oil. Season to taste with salt and pepper and set aside to infuse.

Brush the cod with the remaining oil and coat with the jerk seasoning. Heat a large, heavy-based frying pan and cook the cod, skin-side down, for 5 minutes. Turn the fish over and cook for a further 3 minutes. Transfer to a preheated oven, 150°C (300°F), Gas Mark 2, to rest for about 5 minutes. Garnish the fish with basil and serve with the salsa and a green salad.

For quick crumbed cod, mix together 3 tablespoons each breadcrumbs, torn basil leaves and grated Parmesan cheese, 2 pieces drained and chopped sun-dried tomato, 1 tablespoon olive oil and the grated rind of 1 lemon. Press the mixture over 4 pieces of cod, each 175 g (6 oz), and cook in a preheated oven, 190°C (375°F), Gas Mark 5, for 20 minutes.

salmon fillets with sage & quinoa

Serves **4**
Preparation time **5 minutes**
Cooking time **15 minutes**

200 g (7 oz) **quinoa**
100 g (3½ oz) **butter**, at room
 temperature
8 **sage leaves**, chopped
small bunch of **chives**
grated rind and juice of
 1 **lemon**
4 **salmon fillet steaks**, about
 125 g (4 oz) each
1 tablespoon **olive oil**
salt and **pepper**

Cook the quinoa in unsalted boiling water for about
15 minutes or until cooked but firm.

Meanwhile, mix the butter with the sage, chives and
lemon rind and add salt and pepper to taste.

Rub the salmon steaks with the oil, season with pepper
and cook in a preheated hot griddle pan for about
6 minutes, turning carefully once. Remove and set
aside to rest.

Drain the quinoa, stir in the lemon juice and season
to taste. Spoon on to serving plates and top with the
salmon, topping each piece with a knob of sage butter.

For salmon with tarragon & couscous, replace the
sage leaves with 4 sprigs of tarragon and the quinoa
with 250 g (8 oz) couscous. Soak the couscous in
400 ml (14 fl oz) just-boiled water for 5–8 minutes
until the grains are soft. Fluff the couscous with a fork
and season. Dress with a little lemon juice and olive
oil and serve with the salmon, as above.

cod fillet with tomatoes & rocket

Serves **4**
Preparation time **5 minutes**
Cooking time **12–15 minutes**

4 chunky **cod fillets**, about
150 g (5 oz) each
3 tablespoons **olive oil**
2 **garlic cloves**, chopped
300 g (10 oz) **cherry
tomatoes on the vine**
2 tablespoons **balsamic
vinegar**
4 tablespoons shredded **basil**
125 g (4 oz) **rocket leaves**
salt and **pepper**

Rub the cod fillets all over with 1 tablespoon of the oil and season well. Scatter over the garlic and put the fish in a roasting tray. Arrange the cherry tomatoes alongside and drizzle with the remaining oil, the balsamic vinegar and basil. Season to taste.

Transfer the tray to a preheated oven, 220°C (425°F), Gas Mark 7, and cook for 12–15 minutes until the fish is flaky and the tomatoes roasted.

Serve the cod with the tomatoes and rocket leaves.

For cod with Italian-style salsa, fry the cod fillets for 5–6 minutes until cooked and golden brown. To make the salsa, combine 8 finely chopped sun-dried tomatoes, 2 tablespoons roughly chopped basil leaves, 1 tablespoon drained capers, 1 tablespoon lightly crushed toasted pine nuts and 2 tablespoons olive oil. Serve with a rocket salad.

mussel & lemon curry

Serves **4**
Preparation time **15 minutes**
Cooking time **15 minutes**

1 kg (2 lb) **mussels**, scrubbed
and debearded
125 ml (4 fl oz) **lager**
125 g (4 oz) **unsalted butter**
1 **onion**, chopped
1 **garlic clove**, crushed
2.5 cm (1 inch) **fresh root
ginger**, peeled and grated
1 tablespoon medium **curry
powder**
150 ml (¼ pint) **single cream**
2 tablespoons **lemon juice**
salt and **pepper**
chopped **parsley**, to garnish

Discard any mussels that are broken or do not close immediately when sharply tapped with a knife. Put them in a large saucepan with the lager, cover and cook, shaking the pan frequently, for 4 minutes until all the shells have opened. Discard any that remain closed. Strain, reserve the cooking liquid and keep it warm.

Meanwhile, melt the butter in a large saucepan and fry the onion, garlic, ginger and curry powder, stirring frequently, for 5 minutes. Strain in the reserved mussel liquid and bring to a boil. Boil until reduced by half, whisk in the cream and lemon juice and simmer gently.

Stir in the mussels, warm through and season to taste. Garnish with chopped parsley and serve with crusty bread, if liked.

For prawn & lemon curry with warm lemon naan, substitute the mussels with shelled raw prawns. You will need about 10 prawns per person, cut almost in half down the centre to allow the flavours to penetrate the flesh. Cook in the same way as the mussels for 3–4 minutes until the flesh turns pink. Serve with 4 warm naan breads brushed with lemon butter, made by mixing the rind of 1 lemon with 50 g (2 oz) melted butter.

bream with new potatoes

Serves **4**
Preparation time **5 minutes**
Cooking time **20 minutes**

500 g (1 lb) baby **new potatoes**
3–4 tablespoons **olive oil**
6 tablespoons fresh **mayonnaise**
1 tablespoon chopped **chervil**
½ **garlic clove**, crushed
4 boned **sea bream fillets**
2 tablespoons **lemon juice**
sea salt and **pepper**

Put the new potatoes in a large saucepan with 1–2 tablespoons of the oil. Place over a medium-low heat and cover with a tight-fitting lid. Cook for about 20 minutes, shaking the pan frequently to move the potatoes around. When done, the potatoes should be cooked and crispy golden. Remove from the pan and sprinkle with sea salt.

Meanwhile, mix together the mayonnaise with the chervil and garlic.

Heat the remaining oil in a large frying pan over a medium-high heat. Season the fish with salt and pepper and cook, flesh-side down, for 1 minute before turning carefully and frying for a further 2–3 minutes until the skin is crispy. Squeeze over the lemon juice and serve immediately with the crispy potatoes and garlicky mayonnaise.

For mackerel with horseradish soured cream, replace the chervil and garlic with 2 tablespoons horseradish sauce and the mayonnaise with thick soured cream. Substitute the bream with 4 mackerel fillets, seasoned with salt and pepper and a pinch of chilli powder. Cook in the same way as the bream and serve with new potatoes, as above.

buttery lobster tails with aïoli

Serves **4**
Preparation time **20 minutes**
Cooking time **7–8 minutes**

4 raw **lobster tails**
50 g (2 oz) **butter**
2 tablespoons **garlic-infused oil**
finely grated rind of 1 **lemon**
2 tablespoons chopped **chervil**, plus extra sprigs to garnish
cucumber ribbons, to serve

Aïoli
1 large **egg yolk**
3–4 **garlic cloves**, crushed
1 tablespoon **lemon juice**
175 ml (6 fl oz) **olive oil**
1 tablespoon snipped **chives**
salt and **pepper**

Make the aïoli. With all the ingredients at room temperature, beat the egg yolk in a bowl with the garlic, lemon juice and a large pinch of salt and pepper, either by hand or with an electric whisk. Gradually add the oil, drop by drop, beating constantly until it is all completely incorporated and you have a thick, smooth emulsion. Stir in the chives.

Dot the lobster tails with the butter and drizzle with the garlic oil. Cook the lobster tails, flesh-side up, under a preheated grill for 7–8 minutes until cooked through. Sprinkle with the lemon rind and chopped chervil and serve immediately with cucumber ribbons and the aïoli in small bowls.

For lobster tails with sun-dried tomato sauce, combine 2 tablespoons each of sun-dried tomato paste, mascarpone and pesto with 2 teaspoons finely grated lemon rind and 2 teaspoons lemon juice. Season well.

coconut & coriander mussels

Serves **4**

Preparation time **10 minutes**

Cooking time **15 minutes**

1 tablespoon **vegetable oil**

4 **spring onions**, finely chopped

2½ cm (1 inch) length **galangal** or **fresh root ginger**, shredded

1 **green chilli**, finely chopped

200 ml (7 fl oz) can **coconut milk**

large bunch of **coriander**, chopped, plus extra to garnish

1 tablespoon chopped **Thai basil** (optional)

200 ml (7 fl oz) **fish stock**

2 tablespoons **Thai fish sauce**

2 tablespoons **lime juice**

1 tablespoon **soy sauce**

1 tablespoon **soft brown sugar**

3–4 **lime leaves**, shredded (optional)

1 kg (2 lb) **mussels**, scrubbed and debearded

desiccated coconut, toasted, to garnish (optional)

Heat the oil in a large saucepan and cook the spring onions, galangal or ginger and chilli for 2 minutes until soft. Add the remaining ingredients except the mussels and warm gently until the sugar has dissolved. Turn up the heat and bring up to boiling point, then reduce the heat and simmer gently for 5 minutes to allow the flavours to develop.

Tip the mussels into the coconut sauce and cover with a tight-fitting lid. Cook for 3–4 minutes or until the mussels have opened – discard any that have not.

Spoon into serving bowls with plenty of the juices and sprinkle with extra coriander leaves and desiccated coconut, if using. Serve immediately with steamed jasmine rice or butternut squash.

For coconut & coriander seafood with lime rice, replace the mussels with 500 g (1 lb) fresh or frozen prepared seafood mix and cook as above, but omitting the lime leaves. Cook 250 g (8 oz) rice with the grated rind of 1 lime. Serve the rice in bowls and ladle over the seafood. Serve with prawn crackers.

scallops with citrus dressing

Serves **4**
Preparation time **10 minutes**
Cooking time **7–9 minutes**

16 large **raw prawns**, heads
   removed
24 fresh **scallops**, roe
   removed
1 large ripe but firm **mango**,
   peeled, stoned and cut into
   chunks
125 g (4 oz) mixed **salad
   leaves**

Citrus dressing
juice of ½ **pink grapefruit**
finely grated rind and juice of
   1 lime
1 teaspoon **clear honey**
1 tablespoon **raspberry
   vinegar**
75 ml (3 fl oz) **lemon oil**

Make the citrus dressing by mixing together all the
ingredients in a small bowl.

Poach the prawns in simmering water for 2 minutes
and drain.

Put the scallops, mango and prawns in a bowl and
pour over 3 tablespoons of the dressing. Mix well to
coat before threading them alternately on skewers.

Heat the oil in a large frying pan over a medium heat
and fry the skewers for about 5–7 minutes, turning and
basting occasionally until golden brown and cooked.

Arrange the skewers on plates with salad leaves and
serve with the remaining dressing.

For haloumi & mango kebabs with citrus dressing,
replace the scallops and prawns with 450–500 g
(14½ oz–1 lb) haloumi, cut into cubes. Coat with
the dressing, skewer with the mango and fry, as
above. Alternatively, cook on a barbecue for the same
amount of time until slightly charred.

fried miso cod with pak choi

Serves **4**
Preparation time **10 minutes**,
  plus marinating
Cooking time **13–15 minutes**

4 **cod fillets**, about 175 g
  (6 oz) each
olive oil, for brushing
4 heads **pak choi**, halved
  lengthways and blanched
  in boiling water for
  1–2 minutes

Miso sauce
125 ml (4 fl oz) **miso paste**
50 ml (2 fl oz) **soy sauce**
50 ml (2 fl oz) **sake**
50 ml (2 fl oz) **mirin**
50 g (2 oz) **caster sugar**

Make the miso sauce. Put the miso paste, soy sauce, sake, mirin and sugar into a small saucepan and heat gently until the sugar has dissolved. Simmer gently for about 5 minutes, stirring frequently. Remove from the heat and set aside to cool.

Arrange the cod fillets in a dish into which they fit snugly and cover with the cold miso sauce. Rub the sauce over the fillets so that they are completely covered and leave to marinate for at least 6 hours, preferably overnight.

Heat a frying pan over a medium heat, remove the cod fillets from the miso sauce and cook the fish for about 2–3 minutes. Carefully turn them over and cook for a further 2–3 minutes. Remove and keep warm.

Heat a clean pan. Brush a little oil over the cut side of the pak choi and arrange them, cut-side down, in the pan. Cook for about 2 minutes until hot and lightly charred. Transfer to a serving plate with the cod and serve immediately.

For sesame baby vegetables as an alternative accompaniment, stir-fry 200 g (7 oz) baby corn for 5 minutes then add 100 g (3½ oz) mangetout and cook for a further 3 minutes. Add 1 sliced courgette and cook for a further 3 minutes (total cooking time 11 minutes). Finally, toss the vegetables in 1 tablespoon light soy sauce and 1 teaspoon sesame oil and serve.

teriyaki salmon with noodles

Serves **4**
Preparation time **12 minutes**
Cooking time **15 minutes**

4 boneless, skinless **salmon fillets**, about 150 g (5 oz) each
2 teaspoons **sesame oil**
4 **spring onions**, thinly sliced
350 ml (12 fl oz) hot **vegetable stock**
2 tablespoons **light soy sauce**
50 g (2 oz) **miso paste**
1 tablespoon **mirin** or 1 teaspoon **brown sugar**
300 g (10 oz) ready-cooked **udon noodles**
4 baby heads **pak choi**, halved lengthways

Teriyaki sauce
3 tablespoons **sake**
1 teaspoon **dark soy sauce**
3 tablespoons **light soy sauce**
2 tablespoons **caster sugar**
1 tablespoon **clear honey**
2 tablespoons **mirin** or extra **sugar**

Make the teriyaki sauce. Put all the ingredients in a small saucepan and stir over a medium heat until the sugar has dissolved. Increase the heat a little and simmer for 5 minutes until thickened. Set aside to cool.

Meanwhile, rub the teriyaki sauce over the salmon fillets and arrange them in an ovenproof dish. Cook under a preheated grill for 4–5 minutes on each side, basting occasionally. Remove and set aside.

Heat the sesame oil in a frying pan and stir-fry the spring onions for 2 minutes. Add the stock, soy sauce, miso paste and mirin or sugar, stirring to dissolve. Simmer gently and add the noodles and pak choi and cook for 2 minutes until the leaves have wilted.

Serve immediately topped with the grilled salmon.

For herb-crusted salmon with grilled asparagus, cook 250 g (8 oz) trimmed asparagus spears in boiling water for 5 minutes. Brush one side of each salmon fillet with olive oil. Chop about 25 g (1 oz) parsley and use to coat the salmon, then griddle or fry in olive oil for about 3 minutes on each side. Serve the salmon topped with the asparagus spears and with some crusty bread.

herby chickpea crab cakes

Serves **4**
Preparation time **10 minutes**
Cooking time **7 minutes**

400 g (13 oz) can **chickpeas**, rinsed and drained
2 **spring onions**, thinly sliced
3 tablespoons chopped **parsley**
2 tablespoons chopped **chives**
1 **egg yolk**
1 teaspoon **piri piri sauce**
1 teaspoon **Worcestershire sauce**
2 tablespoons **mayonnaise**
150 g (5 oz) coarse dry **breadcrumbs**
300 g (10 oz) **white crab meat**
2 tablespoons **olive oil**

To serve
125 g (4 oz) **rocket leaves**
4 tablespoons **Aïoli** (see page 116)

Put the chickpeas, spring onions, herbs, egg yolk, piri piri sauce, Worcestershire sauce, mayonnaise and 50 g (2 oz) of the breadcrumbs in a food processor and process briefly. Add the crab meat and pulse quickly to combine, adding more breadcrumbs if the mixture is too wet.

Transfer the mixture to a bowl and form it into 4 large or 8 small patties. Press them into the remaining breadcrumbs until well coated.

Heat the oil in a large frying pan and fry the crab cakes for about 5 minutes, turning carefully once, until crisp and golden. Drain on kitchen paper and serve immediately with rocket leaves and a dollop of aïoli.

For avocado & watercress sauce to serve instead of the aïoli, chop 1 tablespoon capers and 100 g (3½ oz) watercress and mash 1 avocado. Mix together with 200 ml (7 fl oz) Greek yogurt.

squid with lemon mayonnaise

Serves **4**

Preparation time **30 minutes**

Cooking time **9 minutes**

500 g (1 lb) prepared **squid**
50 g (2 oz) **plain flour**
1 tablespoon **paprika**
pinch of **cayenne pepper**
olive oil, for deep-frying
salt and **pepper**

Lemon and herb mayonnaise
2 **egg yolks**
½ teaspoon **wholegrain
mustard**
1 tablespoon **lemon juice**,
plus extra to taste
200 ml (7 fl oz) **light olive oil**
1 tablespoon chopped **flat
leaf parsley**, plus extra
to garnish
1 tablespoon chopped **chervil**
1 tablespoon chopped **chives**
2 tablespoons chopped
watercress
finely grated rind of **1 lemon**
1 small **garlic clove**, crushed
lemon wedges, to serve

Make the mayonnaise. Beat the egg yolks in a bowl
with the mustard and lemon juice. Add the oil, drop by
drop, beating constantly until it is incorporated and you
have a thick, smooth emulsion. Season and stir in the
herbs, watercress, lemon rind and garlic, adding extra
lemon juice to taste. Cover and chill until required.

Wash the squid and pat dry with kitchen paper. Cut
the bodies into rings about 2 cm (¾ inch) thick. Mix
together the flour, paprika and cayenne and season
well. Put the flour in a plastic bag, add the squid rings
and tentacles and shake until they are coated.

Heat the oil in a large frying pan or deep-fat fryer
to 180°C (350°F) or until a cube of bread browns in
20 seconds. Remove about one-third of the squid from
the bag and shake off the excess flour. Carefully drop
the squid into the oil and fry for 2–3 minutes until
golden and crispy, then remove with a slotted spoon.
Drain on kitchen paper and keep them warm while you
cook the rest.

Transfer the squid to 4 serving plates, sprinkle with
parsley and serve immediately with lemon wedges and
Lemon and herb mayonnaise.

For stir-fried squid, prepare and season the squid as
above. Stir-fry in 6 tablespoons olive oil. Remove, drain
and keep warm while you cook 1 sliced onion, 1 sliced
green pepper, 2 crushed garlic cloves, 1 bay leaf,
450 g (14½ oz) chopped tomatoes and 50 g (2 oz)
pitted black olives. Return the squid to the pan, sprinkle
over 4 tablespoons chopped parsley and serve.

creamy smoked fish gratin

Serves **4**
Preparation time **10 minutes**
Cooking time **20 minutes**

4 **plum tomatoes**, chopped
250 g (8 oz) boneless
  smoked trout fillets, skin
  removed
400 g (13 oz) boneless
  smoked haddock fillets,
  skin removed
75 g (3 oz) grated **Gruyère** or
  Emmental cheese
2 tablespoons freshly grated
  Parmesan cheese
2 tablespoons chopped
  chives
200 ml (7 oz) **double cream**
salt and **pepper**
500 g (1 lb) **new potatoes**,
  steamed, to serve (optional)

Arrange the tomatoes over the bottom of 4 lightly buttered individual ovenproof dishes or 1 large ovenproof dish. Cut the fish into chunks and scatter them over the tomatoes. Top with the grated cheeses and chopped chives.

Pour over the cream, place on a baking sheet and cook in a preheated oven, 220°C (425°F), Gas Mark 7, for about 20 minutes until the gratin is bubbling and golden and the fish is cooked.

Serve immediately with steamed new potatoes, if liked.

For creamy cod with prawns, replace the trout and haddock with 450 g (14½ oz) skinless and boneless cod, cut into chunks, and 250 g (8 oz) peeled and cooked prawns. Replace the chives with about 25 g (1 oz) chopped parsley. Finish as above and serve with mashed potatoes with chopped dill added.

vegetarian

spiced pumpkin & spinach soup

Serves **4**
Preparation time **10 minutes**
Cooking time **30–32 minutes**

50 g (2 oz) **butter**
2 tablespoons **olive oil**
1 **onion**, roughly chopped
2 **garlic cloves**, peeled
1.5 kg (3 lb) **pumpkin**, peeled
  and roughly chopped
1 teaspoon **ground coriander**
½ teaspoon **cayenne pepper**
½ teaspoon **ground cinnamon**
¼ teaspoon **ground allspice**
750 ml (1¼ pints) hot
  vegetable stock
150 g (5 oz) **frozen spinach**
salt and **pepper**

To serve
2 tablespoons **pumpkin
  seeds**, lightly toasted
4 teaspoons **pumpkin
  seed oil**

Heat the butter and oil in a large, heatproof casserole and add the onion and garlic. Cook over a medium heat for 5–6 minutes until soft and golden.

Add the pumpkin and continue cooking for a further 8 minutes, stirring frequently, until beginning to soften and turn golden. Add the spices and cook for 2–3 minutes, making sure that the pumpkin is well coated.

Pour in the hot stock and bring to the boil, then reduce the heat, cover and leave to bubble gently for about 15 minutes until the pumpkin is soft.

Use a hand-held blender to liquidize the pumpkin until smooth, then stir in the spinach. Reheat for about 5 minutes until the spinach has melted and the soup is hot. Season to taste.

Spoon the soup into bowls, scatter over the lightly toasted pumpkin seeds and a drizzle of pumpkin oil and serve immediately.

For butternut, spinach & coconut soup, use 500 g (1 lb) butternut squash, peeled, deseeded and cubed, instead of the pumpkin and cook as above. Stir in 200 ml (7 fl oz) coconut milk before serving.

fennel & lemon soup

Serves **4**

Preparation time **20 minutes,**
plus chilling

Cooking time **25 minutes**

50 ml (2 fl oz) **olive oil**

3 fat **spring onions**, chopped

250 g (8 oz) **fennel bulb,**
trimmed, cored and thinly
sliced

1 **potato**, diced

finely grated rind and juice of
1 lemon

about 1.8 litres (3 pints) hot
vegetable stock

pepper

Gremolata

1 small **garlic clove**, finely
chopped

finely grated rind of **1 lemon**

4 tablespoons chopped
parsley

16 **black olives**, pitted
and chopped

Heat the oil in a large saucepan, add the spring onions and cook for 5 minutes or until beginning to soften. Add the fennel, potato and lemon rind and cook for 5 minutes until the fennel begins to soften. Pour in the stock and bring to the boil. Reduce the heat, cover and simmer for about 15 minutes or until the ingredients are tender.

Meanwhile, make the gremolata. Mix together the garlic, lemon rind and parsley, then stir the chopped olives into the mixture. Cover and chill.

Liquidize the soup in a food processor or blender and pass it through a sieve. The soup should not be too thick, so add more stock if necessary. Return it to the rinsed pan and warm through. Taste and season with pepper and plenty of lemon juice. Pour into warm bowls and sprinkle each serving with gremolata, to be stirred in before eating. Serve with slices of toasted crusty bread, if liked.

For butter bean & fennel soup, heat 900 ml (1½ pints) vegetable stock with 2 trimmed, cored and sliced fennel bulbs, 1 sliced onion, 1 sliced carrot, 1 sliced courgette and 2 crushed garlic cloves. Boil gently for 20 minutes, then add 2 x 400 g (13½ oz) cans butter beans and a 400 g (13½ oz) can chopped tomatoes. Heat, stir in 2 tablespoons chopped sage, process to blend and serve.

broad bean salad

Serves **4**
Preparation time **10 minutes**
Cooking time **20 minutes**

2 **aubergines**, thinly sliced
   into rounds
2 **yellow courgettes**, thinly
   sliced lengthways
4–6 tablespoons **olive oil**
300 g (10 oz) **frozen baby
   broad beans**
1 tablespoon chopped **dill**
1 tablespoon chopped **mint**
1 small **fennel bulb**, thinly
   sliced
200 g (7 oz) **feta cheese**,
   crumbled
salt and **pepper**
mint leaves, to garnish
1 **lemon**, cut into wedges,
   to serve

Brush the aubergines and courgettes with oil and cook in a griddle pan for 2–3 minutes on each side until soft and golden. You will have to do this in several batches.

Cook the broad beans in boiling water until tender. Drain and toss with 1 tablespoon of the oil, the herbs and plenty of seasoning.

Leave the broad beans, aubergines and courgettes to cool before assembling or serve them as a warm salad. Arrange the aubergine and courgette slices on serving plates, scatter over the broad beans and sliced fennel and then the feta. Sprinkle over a few mint leaves and serve with lemon wedges.

For broad bean & celeriac salad, replace the courgettes with 2 thinly sliced red peppers and the fennel with 250 g (8 oz) coarsely grated celeriac.

papaya & lime salad

Serves **4**
Preparation time **15 minutes**
Cooking time **3–5 minutes**

3 firm, ripe **papayas**
2 **limes**
2 teaspoons **light brown sugar**
50 g (2 oz) **blanched almonds**, toasted
lime wedges, to garnish

Cut the papayas in half, scoop out the seeds and discard. Peel the halves, roughly dice the flesh and place in a bowl.

Finely grate the rind of both limes, then squeeze one of the limes and reserve the juice. Cut the pith off the second lime and segment the flesh over the bowl of diced papaya to catch the juice. Add the lime segments and grated rind to the papaya.

Pour the lime juice into a small saucepan with the sugar and heat gently until the sugar has dissolved. Remove from the heat and leave to cool.

Pour the cooled lime juice over the fruit and toss thoroughly. Add the toasted almonds and serve with lime wedges.

For papaya & lime yogurt, use 1 papaya and 1 lime. Prepare the papaya as above, omitting the segments and syrup. Chop the almonds. Mix with 400 g (13 oz) thick Greek yogurt and serve for breakfast with muesli or as a simple pudding, topped with granola. It is also very good as a topping for waffles.

vegetable & cheese wrap

Serves **4**

Preparation time **10 minutes**

Cooking time **6–8 minutes**

200 g (7 oz) **soft, mild goats' cheese**

8 medium-sized **soft tortilla wraps**

16 **basil leaves**

150 g (5 oz) **grilled artichokes in oil**, drained

150 g (5 oz) **grilled aubergines in oil**, drained

150 g (5 oz) **grilled peppers in oil**, drained

8 **sun-dried tomatoes**

50 g (2 oz) **pine nuts**, lightly toasted

75 g (3 oz) **wild rocket**

4 tablespoons **Parmesan cheese** shavings (optional)

Spread the cheese over the tortillas and arrange the basil leaves lengthways in the centre of each wrap. Top with the vegetables and finish with the pine nuts, rocket and Parmesan shavings, if used.

Roll up each tortilla by bringing in the sides and then rolling the wrap so that the sides are closed and the filling is concealed.

Heat a large, dry, griddle pan or frying pan over a medium heat. Cook the wraps for about 6–8 minutes, turning frequently. Remove from the heat, cut each one diagonally and serve immediately.

For cheese & tomato wraps with peppers, replace the goats' cheese with a soft cheese with herbs and garlic. Omit the artichokes and aubergines and replace the sun-dried tomatoes with 400 g (13 oz) fresh cherry tomatoes, which you should halve.

stuffed sweet potato melt

Serves **4**
Preparation time **10 minutes**
Cooking time **50 minutes**

4 sweet potatoes
350 g (11½ oz) **taleggio cheese**, sliced
½ teaspoon **dried thyme**
sprigs of **parsley**, to garnish

Caramelized onions
75 ml (3 fl oz) **vegetable oil**
6 large **onions**, sliced
4 tablespoons **white wine**
3 tablespoons **white wine vinegar**
1 tablespoon **soft brown sugar**
1 teaspoon **dried thyme**
salt and **pepper**

Prick the sweet potatoes with a sharp knife and put them in a preheated oven, 220°C (425°F), Gas Mark 7, for about 45 minutes or until the flesh is soft when tested with a knife.

Meanwhile, make the caramelized onions. Heat the oil in a large frying pan over a low heat and add all the remaining ingredients. Cook slowly, stirring occasionally, for about 30 minutes until the onions are nut brown and soft.

Remove the potatoes from the oven and put them on a baking sheet. Carefully slice the potatoes in half and pile over the caramelized onions. Top with the sliced taleggio and a sprinkling of thyme and cook under a preheated hot grill for 4–5 minutes until bubbling and beginning to brown.

Garnish with sprigs of parsley and serve immediately with a crisp green salad and a dollop of soured cream, if liked.

For polenta with caramelized onions & goats' cheese rounds, cut 2 x 500 g (1 lb) packets of ready-made polenta into 8 slices and cut 2 x 100 g (3½ oz) goats' cheeses into 4 slices each. Grill the polenta slices on one side. Turn them over and top each one with some caramelized onions, prepared as above, and 1 slice of goats' cheese. Return to the grill for about 5 minutes, until the cheese is brown on top and soft.

spinach & sweet potato cakes

Serves **4**

Preparation time **35 minutes**, plus infusing

Cooking time **about 40 minutes**

500 g (1 lb) **sweet potatoes**, peeled and cut into chunks

125 g (4 oz) **spinach leaves**

4–5 **spring onions**, finely sliced

olive oil, for deep-frying

3 tablespoons **sesame seeds**

4 tablespoons **plain flour**

salt and **pepper**

Red chilli & coconut dip

200 ml (7 fl oz) **coconut cream**

2 **red chillies**, deseeded and finely chopped

1 **lemon grass stalk**, thinly sliced

3 **kaffir lime leaves**, shredded

small bunch of fresh **coriander**, chopped

2 tablespoons **sesame oil**

To garnish

lime wedges

spring onions, shredded

Cook the sweet potatoes in lightly salted boiling water for about 20 minutes or until tender. Drain, then return them to the pan and place over a low heat for 1 minute, stirring constantly, so the excess moisture evaporates. Lightly mash the potatoes with a fork.

Meanwhile, put the spinach in a colander and pour over a kettle of boiling water. Refresh the spinach in cold water and squeeze dry. Stir the wilted spinach into the potatoes, then add the spring onions. Season well and set aside.

Make the dip. Gently warm the coconut cream in a pan with the chillies, lemon grass and lime leaves for about 10 minutes. Don't let it boil. Set aside to infuse.

Heat the oil in a large pan or deep-fat fryer to 180°C (350°F) or until a cube of bread browns in 20 seconds. Use your hands to form the potato mixture into 12 cakes. Mix together the sesame seeds and flour and sprinkle over the cakes, then carefully lower them into the oil and fry in batches for about 3 minutes until they are golden and crispy. Drain on kitchen paper and keep warm while you cook the rest.

Stir the coriander and sesame oil into the dip and pour it into 4 individual dishes. Serve immediately with the potato cakes, garnished with lime wedges and spring onions.

For sage-seasoned spinach & sweet potato cakes with apple sauce, shred 6 large fresh sage leaves and add to the potato cakes. Cook 400 g (13 oz) cooking apples and beat to a purée with 3–4 tablespoons sugar. Add 25 g melted butter and the rind of 1 lemon. Serve the hot cakes as a starter with the apple sauce.

mushroom & broccoli pie

Serves **4**
Preparation time **8 minutes**
Cooking time **30 minutes**

350 g (11½ oz) **broccoli florets**
3 tablespoons **olive oil**
350 g (11½ oz) **mushrooms**, trimmed and thickly sliced
150 g (5 oz) **Gorgonzola cheese**
3 tablespoons **mascarpone cheese**
4 tablespoons **crème fraîche**
2 tablespoons chopped **chives**
1 large sheet ready-rolled **puff pastry** (thawed if frozen)
1 **egg**, lightly beaten
salt and **pepper**

Cook the broccoli in lightly salted boiling water for about 2 minutes or until the florets are just beginning to soften.

Meanwhile, heat the oil in a large frying pan and cook the mushrooms over a medium heat, stirring occasionally, for about 5 minutes. Stir in the Gorgonzola, mascarpone and crème fraîche. Add the drained broccoli florets and the chives, season and tip into 4 individual ovenproof dishes or 1 large rectangular ovenproof dish.

Lay the pastry over the filling, pressing it to the sides of the dish to seal. Brush the top with beaten egg and cut two slits. Cook in a preheated oven, 220°C (425°F), Gas Mark 7, for about 25 minutes until the pastry is crisp and golden. Serve immediately.

For puff-crust cauliflower cheese pie, use 450 g (14½ oz) cauliflower florets instead of the broccoli and 200 g (7 oz) grated strong Cheddar cheese instead of the Gorgonzola. Omit the mushrooms.

cumin lentils with yogurt dressing

Serves **4**
Preparation time **10 minutes**
Cooking time **13 minutes**

4 tablespoons **olive oil**
2 **red onions**, thinly sliced
2 **garlic cloves**, chopped
2 teaspoon **cumin seeds**
500 g (1 lb) cooked **Puy lentils**
125 g (4 oz) **peppery leaves**, such as beetroot or rocket
1 large raw **beetroot**, peeled and coarsely grated
1 **Granny Smith apple**, peeled and coarsely grated (optional)
lemon juice, to serve
salt and **pepper**

Yogurt dressing
300 ml (½ pint) **Greek yogurt**
2 tablespoons **lemon juice**
½ teaspoon **ground cumin**
15 g (½ oz) **mint leaves**, chopped

Heat the oil in a frying pan and fry the red onions over a medium heat for about 8 minutes until soft and golden. Add the garlic and cumin seeds and cook for a further 5 minutes.

Mix the onion mixture into the lentils, season well and leave to cool.

Make the dressing by mixing together the ingredients in a small bowl.

Serve the cooled lentils on a bed of leaves, with the grated beetroot and apple (if used), a couple of spoonfuls of minty yogurt and a generous squeeze of lemon juice.

For cumin chickpeas with apricots, use 2 x 425 g (14 oz) cans chickpeas instead of the lentils. Chop and add 100 g (3½ oz) ready-to-eat dried apricots to replace the beetroot and apple.

asparagus with tarragon dressing

Serves **4**
Preparation time **20 minutes**
Cooking time **about 5 minutes**

3 tablespoons **olive oil** (optional)
500 g (1 lb) **asparagus**
750 g (1½ lb) **rocket** or other **salad leaves**
2 **green onions**, finely sliced
4 **radishes**, thinly sliced
salt and **pepper**

Tarragon & lemon dressing
finely grated rind of 2 **lemons**
4 tablespoons **tarragon vinegar**
2 tablespoons chopped **tarragon**
½ teaspoon **Dijon mustard**
pinch of **caster sugar**
150 ml (¼ pint) **olive oil**

To garnish
roughly chopped **herbs**, such as tarragon, parsley, chervil or dill
thin strips of **lemon rind**

Make the dressing. Combine the lemon rind, vinegar, tarragon, mustard and sugar in a small bowl and season to taste. Stir to mix, then gradually whisk in the oil. Alternatively, place all the ingredients in a screw-top jar and shake well to combine. Set aside.

Heat the oil (if used) in a large frying pan. Add the asparagus in a single layer and cook for about 5 minutes, turning occasionally. (The asparagus should be tender when pierced with the tip of a sharp knife and lightly patched with brown.)

Transfer the asparagus to a shallow dish and sprinkle with salt and pepper. Cover with the dressing, toss gently and leave to stand for 5 minutes.

Arrange the salad leaves in a serving dish, sprinkle over the onions and radishes and pile the asparagus in the centre of the leaves. Garnish with chopped herbs and thin strips of lemon rind. Serve on its own with bread or as an accompaniment to a main dish.

For garlic & mustard dressing as an alternative to tarragon and lemon, place in a screw-top jar 1 finely chopped small garlic clove, 1 finely chopped small shallot, 2 tablespoons wholegrain mustard, a pinch each of salt, pepper and sugar, 125 ml (4 fl oz) olive oil and 2–3 tablespoons shallot or red wine vinegar. Place the lid on the jar and shake until the ingredients are well combined. Serve drizzled over the asparagus.

curried dhal with spinach

Serves **4**
Preparation time **5 minutes**
Cooking time **15 minutes**

500 g (1 lb) **red lentils**
100 g (3½ oz) **butter**
1 **onion**, sliced
1 **garlic clove**, crushed
2 tablespoons **cider vinegar**
1 tablespoons **ground coriander**
1 teaspoon **turmeric**
1 teaspoon **ground cumin**
2 tablespoons medium **curry powder**
½ teaspoon **chilli powder**
200 g (7 oz) chopped **spinach**
1 teaspoon **garam masala**
salt and **pepper**

To serve
8 **chapattis**
mango chutney

Cook the lentils in plenty of unsalted boiling water for about 12 minutes or until they are soft but holding their shape.

Meanwhile, melt the butter in a saucepan and gently cook the onion for about 8 minutes until it is softened but not coloured. Add the garlic and cook for 1 minute, then stir in the vinegar and all the spices except the garam masala and fry gently for 2 minutes.

Drain the lentils and stir them into the spice mix with the chopped spinach. Heat until the spinach has wilted and the lentils are hot. Season to taste, stir in the garam masala and serve immediately with plenty of chapattis and mango chutney.

For potato & spinach curry, dice 500 g (1 lb) potatoes and cook them for 10 minutes, until just tender and substitute for the lentils. Increase the quantity of spinach to 500 g (1 lb). Serve sprinkled with toasted, chopped cashew nuts.

herby chickpea fatoush

Serves **4**
Preparation time **15 minutes**
Cooking time **4 minutes**

3 **pitta breads**
1 **garlic clove**, peeled and
  halved
1 **green pepper**, cored,
  deseeded and thinly sliced
10–12 **radishes**, thinly sliced
400 g (13 oz) can **chickpeas**,
  rinsed and drained
15 g (½ oz) **parsley**, chopped
15 g (½ oz) **mint**, chopped
2 ripe **tomatoes**, deseeded
  and sliced
½ **red onion**, finely chopped,
  or 4 **spring onions**, finely
  sliced
½ **cucumber**, deseeded
  and diced
75 ml (3 fl oz) **olive oil**
3 tablespoons **lemon juice**
1 tablespoon **tahini** (optional)
1 teaspoon **sumac** (optional)
8 cos (romaine) **lettuce**
  leaves, to serve

Heat a griddle pan and toast the pitta breads for 2 minutes on each side until crisp and slightly charred. Remove from the pan and rub immediately with the cut garlic. Cut the bread into squares.

Combine the pitta cubes with the green pepper, radishes, chickpeas, parsley, mint, tomatoes, onion and cucumber. Pour over the oil and lemon juice and stir in the tahini (if used). Mix until the salad is well coated. Tip into a serving dish and scatter over the sumac (if used).

Put 2 lettuce leaves on each serving plate and let people help themselves to the fatoush.

For cannellini & French bread salad, replace the pitta bread with French bread cubes, baked in a preheated oven, 180°C (350°F), Gas Mark 4, for about 15 minutes until crisp and browning. Use cannellini beans instead of chickpeas and replace the tahini with 2 tablespoons pesto. Omit the sumac and garlic.

tabbouleh with fruit & nuts

Serves **4**
Preparation time **10 minutes**,
  plus soaking

150 g (5 oz) **bulgar wheat**
75 g (3 oz) **unsalted, shelled pistachio nuts**
1 small **red onion**, finely chopped
3 **garlic cloves**, crushed
25 g (1 oz) **flat leaf parsley**, chopped
15 g (½ oz) **mint**, chopped
finely grated rind and juice of
  1 **lemon** or **lime**
150 g (5 oz) **ready-to-eat prunes**, sliced
4 tablespoons **olive oil**
salt and **pepper**

Put the bulgar wheat in a bowl, cover with plenty of boiling water and leave to soak for 15 minutes.

Meanwhile, put the nuts in a separate bowl and cover with boiling water. Leave to stand for 1 minute, then drain. Rub the nuts between several thicknesses of kitchen paper to remove most of the skins, then peel away any remaining skins with your fingers.

Mix the nuts with the onion, garlic, parsley, mint, lemon or lime rind and juice and prunes in a large bowl.

Drain the bulgar wheat thoroughly in a sieve, pressing out as much moisture as possible with the back of a spoon. Add to the other ingredients with the oil and toss together. Season to taste with salt and pepper and chill until ready to serve.

For classic tabbouleh, omit the nuts and prunes and add 6 chopped tomatoes and 50 g (2 oz) chopped black olives. Use only 2 garlic cloves and be sure to use a lemon not a lime.

haloumi with cucumber salad

Serves **4**
Preparation time **10 minutes**
Cooking time **5–6 minutes**

1 **cucumber**, sliced into long,
  thin ribbons
20 Greek-style pitted **black
  olives**
2 tablespoons chopped
  parsley
2 tablespoons chopped **mint**
1 **green pepper**, cored,
  deseeded and diced
8 **radishes**, sliced into thin
  batons
2 **spring onions**, thinly sliced
  (optional)
4 tablespoons **olive oil**
2 tablespoons **lemon juice**
8 thick slices of **country-style
  bread**
250 g (8 oz) **haloumi cheese**,
  sliced
1 tablespoon finely grated
  lemon rind
pepper

Combine the cucumber, olives, herbs, green pepper, radishes and spring onions (if used) with 3 tablespoons of the oil and the lemon juice. Season with pepper and set aside.

Heat a frying pan or griddle pan to medium-hot and toast the bread for 1–2 minutes on each side until golden and slightly charred. Toss the cheese in the remaining oil and lemon rind and season with pepper, add to the pan and cook for 3–4 minutes, turning once, until golden.

Put a cheese slice on top of each piece of toast and serve with the salad.

For tomato, mint & avocado salad, roughly chop 4 ripe plum tomatoes, very finely slice ½ red onion and roughly dice 1 ripe but firm avocado. Gently toss all the ingredients in 2 tablespoons olive oil, with 2 tablespoons chopped fresh mint and the juice of ½ lemon.

orange & avocado salad

Serves **4**
Preparation time **15 minutes**

4 large juicy **oranges**
2 small ripe **avocados**, peeled
  and stoned
2 teaspoons **cardamom pods**
3 tablespoons **light olive oil**
1 tablespoon **clear honey**
pinch of **ground allspice**
2 teaspoons **lemon juice**
salt and **pepper**
sprigs of **watercress**,
  to garnish

Cut the skin and the white membrane off the oranges. Working over a bowl to catch the juice, cut between the membranes to remove the segments. Slice the avocados and toss gently with the orange segments. Pile on to serving plates.

Reserve a few whole cardamom pods for garnishing. Crush the remainder using a mortar and pestle to extract the seeds or place them in a small bowl and crush with the end of a rolling pin. Pick out and discard the pods.

Mix the seeds with the oil, honey, allspice and lemon juice. Season to taste and stir in the reserved orange juice. Garnish the salads with sprigs of watercress and the reserved cardamom pods and serve with the dressing spooned over the top.

For orange & walnut salad, separate the segments from 2 large oranges as above and mix them with 1 crushed garlic clove, 75 g (3 oz) chopped walnut halves and 4 thinly sliced heads of chicory. Stir in 3 tablespoons walnut oil and ½ teaspoon caster sugar. Decorate with whole walnuts and serve.

asparagus & mangetout stir-fry

Serves **4**
Preparation time **10 minutes**
Cooking time **7–9 minutes**

2 tablespoons **vegetable oil**
100 g (3½ oz) **fresh root ginger**, peeled and thinly shredded
2 large **garlic cloves**, thinly sliced
4 **spring onions**, diagonally sliced
250 g (8 oz) thin **asparagus spears**, cut into 3 cm (1¼ inch) lengths
150 g (5 oz) **mangetout**, cut in half diagonally
150 g (5 oz) **bean sprouts**
3 tablespoons **light soy sauce**

To serve
steamed rice
extra **soy sauce** (optional)

Heat a large wok until it is smoking then add the oil. Stir-fry the ginger and garlic for 30 seconds, add the spring onions and cook for a further 30 seconds. Add the asparagus and cook, stirring frequently, for another 3–4 minutes.

Add the mangetout and cook for 2–3 minutes until the vegetables are still crunchy but beginning to soften. Finally, add the bean sprouts and toss in the hot oil for 1–2 minutes before pouring in the soy sauce and removing from the heat.

Serve immediately with steamed rice and extra soy sauce, if liked.

For stir-fried vegetable omelettes, for each omelette, beat together 3 eggs with 2 tablespoons water and seasoning. Cook in a frying pan until lightly set (see page 166 for instructions). Top with a quarter of the cooked vegetables and fold in half. Set aside to keep warm and make three more.

pea & leek omelette

Serves **4**
Preparation time **5–6 minutes**
Cooking time **19–22 minutes**

250 g (8 oz) baby **new potatoes**
75 g (3 oz) **butter**
1 tablespoon **olive oil**
500 g (1 lb) **leeks**, trimmed, cleaned and cut into 1 cm (½ inch) slices
200 g (7 oz) frozen or fresh **peas**
6 **eggs**
150 ml (5 fl oz) **milk**
2 tablespoons chopped **chives**
125 g (4 oz) **soft garlic and chive cheese**
salt and **pepper**

To serve
125 g (4 oz) **salad leaves**
4 tablespoons ready-made **salad dressing**

Cook the potatoes in boiling water for about 10 minutes or until cooked but still firm.

Meanwhile, melt the butter with the oil in a large frying pan, add the leeks, cover and cook, stirring frequently, for 8–10 minutes or until soft. Stir in the peas.

Drain the potatoes, cut them into quarters and add to the frying pan. Continue cooking for 2–3 minutes.

Whisk the eggs with the milk and chives, season well and pour into the frying pan. Move around with a spatula so that the vegetables are well coated and the egg begins to cook. Crumble the cheese on top and leave over a medium heat for 2–3 minutes until the egg becomes firm.

Place under a preheated hot grill for 3–4 minutes until the omelette is completely set and the top is golden brown. Serve in thick slices with a prepared salad and ready-made dressing.

For quick herb salad dressing, whisk together 6 tablespoons olive oil, 2 tablespoons wine vinegar, 3 tablespoons chopped parsley, ½ grated small onion, ½ teaspoon mustard, ¼ teaspoon caster sugar and a little ground coriander. Season to taste.

wild rice & goats' cheese salad

Serves **4**
Preparation time **10 minutes**
Cooking time **about
15 minutes**

250 g (8 oz) mixed **long grain
and wild rice**
100 g (3½ oz) **fine green
beans**
4 tablespoons **olive oil**
3 **red onions**, thinly sliced
150 ml (5 fl oz) **balsamic
vinegar**
1 teaspoon chopped **thyme**
125 g (4 oz) **goats' cheese**,
sliced
8 **baby plum tomatoes**,
halved
small bunch of **basil**
salt and **pepper**

Cook the rice in lightly salted boiling water for about 15 minutes until tender or according to the instructions on the packet. Add the green beans for the final 2 minutes of cooking. Drain and set aside.

Meanwhile, heat the oil in a large frying pan and cook the onions gently for about 12 minutes or until soft and golden. Add the balsamic vinegar and thyme, season with salt and pepper and allow to bubble gently for 2–3 minutes until the mixture thickens slightly.

Stir the onions into the rice and beans and leave to cool. Once cool, scatter over the cheese, tomatoes and basil leaves and serve.

For pearl barley salad with smoked cheese, replace the rice with the same quantity of pearl barley and cook in boiling water for 25–35 minutes until tender, then drain. Substitute the goats' cheese for diced smoked cheese.

potato gratin with chicory

Serves **4**
Preparation time **10 minutes**
Cooking time **43–45 minutes**

1.5 kg (3 lb) **floury potatoes,**
  peeled and cut into 3–4 mm
  (about ¼ inch) sliced
50 g (2 oz) **butter**
1 tablespoon **olive oil**
1 **onion**, sliced
3 **garlic cloves**, chopped
200 g (7 oz) **Cheddar**
  cheese, grated
400 ml (14 fl oz) **double**
  cream or full-fat **crème**
  fraîche
375 g (12 oz) **Reblochon** or
  Brie cheese, sliced
salt and **pepper**

To serve
3–4 heads **chicory**, separated
ready-made **French dressing**

Cook the potatoes in lightly salted boiling water for 10 minutes, then drain.

Melt the butter with the oil in a medium saucepan and cook the onion for about 5 minutes, or until soft and golden. Add the garlic and cook for a further 2 minutes.

Add the grated cheese and cream or crème fraîche. Stir until the mixture is hot and the cheese has melted. Season to taste.

Arrange half the potatoes in a lightly buttered, shallow, ovenproof dish. Place half the cheese slices over the potatoes and pour over half the cheese sauce. Cover with the remaining potato slices, the rest of the cheese sauce and top with the remaining cheese slices.

Cook in a preheated oven, 220°C (425°F), Gas Mark 7, for 30–35 minutes until bubbling and golden brown. Serve immediately with the chicory and dressing.

For Italian-style gratin, use 150 g (5 oz) grated pecorino and 400 g (13 oz) fontina for the hard and soft cheeses. Sprinkle over a teaspoon of dried Italian herbs and add 1 teaspoon finely chopped rosemary before baking.

beetroot & squash spaghetti

Serves **4**
Preparation time **8 minutes**
Cooking time **10 minutes**

300 g (10 oz) dried **spaghetti**
  or **fusilli**
150 g (5 oz) **fine green**
  beans
500 g (1 lb) **butternut**
  squash, peeled, deseeded
  and cut into 1 cm (½ inch)
  dice
4 tablespoons **olive oil**
500 g (1 lb) raw **beetroot**, cut
  into 1 cm (½ inch) dice
50 g (2 oz) **walnuts**, crushed
150 g (5 oz) **goats' cheese**,
  diced
2 tablespoons **lemon juice**
freshly grated **Parmesan**
  cheese, to serve (optional)

Cook the pasta in lightly salted boiling water for 10 minutes or until just cooked. Add the beans and squash for the final 2 minutes of cooking time.

Meanwhile, heat the oil in a large frying pan, add the beetroot and cook, stirring occasionally, for 10 minutes until cooked but still firm.

Toss the drained pasta mixture with the beetroot, walnuts and goats' cheese. Squeeze over the lemon juice and serve immediately with a bowl of Parmesan, if liked.

For baby carrot & squash spaghetti, replace the beetroot with the same quantity of baby carrots, cooked in boiling water for about 5 minutes, until tender. Roast the butternut squash with 4 garlic cloves and the oil in a preheated oven, 240°C (475°F), Gas Mark 9, for about 40 minutes or until softened. Replace the goats' cheese with havarti or dolcelatte.

italian warm bean linguine

Serves **4**
Preparation time **10 minutes**
Cooking time **12 minutes**

400 g (13 oz) **dried linguine**
4 tablespoons **olive oil**, plus
   extra to drizzle (optional)
1 **red onion**, finely chopped
2 **celery sticks**, chopped
1 **courgette**, grated
1 **garlic clove**, chopped
400 g (13 oz) can **borlotti
   beans**, rinsed and drained
4 tablespoons chopped
   parsley, plus extra to garnish
6 **sun-dried tomatoes**,
   chopped
finely grated rind and juice
   of 1 **lemon**

Cook the pasta in lightly salted boiling water for
10 minutes or according to the instructions on the
packet. Drain and set aside and keep warm.

Meanwhile, heat the oil in a frying pan over a medium
heat, add the onion and celery and cook for about
8 minutes or until softened and beginning to colour.
Add the courgette and garlic and stir-fry for a further
1–2 minutes.

Add the beans to the pan and stir in the parsley,
chopped tomatoes and lemon rind and juice. Cook
for 1 minute, then remove from the heat.

Stir the vegetables into the pasta and serve
immediately, drizzled with extra olive oil and parsley,
if liked.

For crunchy asparagus linguine, whiz 2–3 slices
of white bread in a food processor to make
breadcrumbs. Mix well with the finely grated zest
of 1 lemon, 1 crushed garlic clove, 2 tablespoons
finely grated Parmesan and 2 tablespoons pine nuts,
season before toasting in a large frying pan with
1 tablespoon olive oil for 3–4 minutes until golden
and crunchy. Slice 125 g (4 oz) fine asparagus tips
lengthways and blanch in boiling water for 1 minute,
drain and toss with the linguine, the juice of 1 lemon
and plenty of black pepper. Serve scattered with the
crunchy breadcrumb mixture.

zesty quinoa salad

Serves **4**
Preparation time **15 minutes**
Cooking time **15–20 minutes**

150 g (5 oz) **quinoa**, rinsed
1 small **yellow pepper**, cored, deseeded and diced
1 small **red pepper**, cored, deseeded and diced
4 **spring onions**, sliced
⅓ **cucumber**, deseeded and diced
½ **fennel bulb**, finely diced
2 tablespoons finely chopped **curly parsley**
2 tablespoons finely chopped **mint**
2 tablespoons finely chopped **coriander**
2 tablespoons **sunflower seeds**
juice and finely grated rind of **2 limes**
8 **physalis**, quartered

Dressing
4 teaspoons **harissa paste**
juice and finely grated rind of **2 limes**
8 tablespoons **sunflower oil**
salt and **pepper**

Put the quinoa in a pan of cold water, bring to the boil and cook for 15–20 minutes or until the quinoa is translucent and just cooked. Drain and rinse thoroughly in cold water.

Meanwhile, make the dressing by mixing together the harissa paste, lime juice and rind and oil. Season to taste and set aside.

Mix the cooked quinoa with the prepared vegetables and herbs, 1 tablespoon of the sunflower seeds and the lime juice and rind.

Scatter over the physalis and the remaining sunflower seeds and serve with the dressing.

For baked potatoes with quinoa salad, coat 4 large potatoes, about 400 g each, with olive oil and salt, prick all over with a fork and bake in a preheated oven, 220°C (425°F), Gas Mark 7, for about an hour, until the skins are crisp and a skewer slides in easily. Make the salad as above, omitting the sunflower seeds, limes and physalis. Mix 200 ml (7 fl oz) soured cream with 2 tablespoons chopped chives and a little nutmeg. Fill the potatoes with the salad and top with the soured cream instead of the dressing.

feta & watermelon salad

Serves **4**
Preparation time **10 minutes**
Cooking time **2 minutes**

1 tablespoon **black sesame seeds**
500 g (1 lb) **watermelon**, peeled, deseeded and diced
175 g (6 oz) **feta cheese**, diced
875 g (1¾ lb) **rocket**
sprigs of **mint**, **parsley** and **coriander**
6 tablespoons **olive oil**
1 tablespoon **orange flower water**
1½ tablespoons **lemon juice**
1 teaspoon **pomegranate syrup** (optional)
½ teaspoon **caster sugar**
salt and **pepper**

Heat a frying pan and dry-fry the sesame seeds for 2 minutes until aromatic, then set aside.

Arrange the watermelon and feta on a large plate with the rocket and herbs.

Whisk together the oil, orange flower water, lemon juice, pomegranate syrup (if used) and sugar. Season to taste with salt and pepper, then drizzle over the salad. Scatter over the sesame seeds and serve with toasted pitta bread.

For quick feta & tomato salad, mix 500 g (1 lb) skinned and chopped tomatoes with 250 g (8 oz) cubed feta and 50 g (2 oz) pitted black olives. Drizzle over a mixture of 3 tablespoons olive oil, 2 chopped garlic cloves and ½ teaspoon caster sugar. Season with plenty of black pepper and serve.

grilled polenta & cheese bake

Serves **4**
Preparation time **8 minutes**
Cooking time **25–30 minutes**

200 g (7 oz) **roasted red peppers in olive oil**
1 kg (2 lb) ready-made, firm **polenta**, cut into 5 mm (¼ inch) slices
150 g (5 oz) **fontina cheese**, grated
150 g (5 oz) **pecorino cheese**, grated
1 **garlic clove**, chopped
350 ml (12 fl oz) **passata**
1 teaspoon finely grated **lemon rind**
pinch of **caster sugar**
small bunch of **basil**, shredded, plus extra whole leaves to garnish
salt and **pepper**

Drain and slice the red peppers, reserving 3 tablespoons of the oil.

Arrange half the polenta slices in a lightly buttered ovenproof dish and scatter over half the sliced peppers and cheeses.

Repeat the layers and cook in a preheated oven, 240°C (475°F), Gas Mark 9, for 15 minutes.

Meanwhile, heat the oil from the peppers in a pan and fry the garlic over a medium heat until soft and beginning to turn golden. Stir in the remaining ingredients, season to taste and bring to the boil, then reduce the heat and leave to bubble gently for 15–20 minutes.

Put the polenta bake under a preheated hot grill for 5 minutes to brown the top. Garnish with basil leaves and serve immediately with the tomato sauce.

For semolina gnocchi, add 250 g (8 oz) semolina to 900 ml (1½ pints) boiling milk, reduce the heat and simmer for 5 minutes, stirring constantly with a whisk until thick. Add a little butter then pour into a 1 kg (2 lb) loaf tin. Cook in a preheated oven, 180°C (350°F), Gas Mark 4, until firm, and slice. Layer and grill as above.

desserts

strawberry jellies

Serves **6**

Preparation time **10 minutes**, plus standing and chilling

Cooking time **5 minutes**

450 g (14½ oz) **strawberries**, hulled

100 g (3½ oz) **caster sugar**

500 ml (17 fl oz) **white grape juice**

2 sachets of **powdered gelatine** or 6 **gelatine leaves**

75 ml (3 fl oz) **crème de cassis** (optional)

Roughly chop three-quarters of the strawberries and put them in a food processor or blender with 300 ml (½ pint) boiling water and the sugar. Blend until smooth, then pour the mixture into a sieve set over a bowl and stir to allow the liquid to drip through.

Pour 200 ml (7 fl oz) of the grape juice into a heatproof bowl, sprinkle over the gelatine and allow to stand for 10 minutes. Place the bowl over a saucepan of simmering water and stir until the gelatine has dissolved. Leave to cool, then stir in the cassis (if used), strawberry liquid and the remaining grape juice.

Arrange the remaining strawberries in 6 large wine glasses, pour over the liquid and chill until the jelly has set.

For raspberry champagne jellies, substitute the strawberries for raspberries and omit the cassis. Dissolve the gelatine in only 100 ml (3½ fl oz) grape juice and, when cool, stir in 400 ml (14 fl oz) sparkling white wine. Finish as above.

chocolate, date & almond panini

Serves **4**

Preparation time **10 minutes**, plus cooling

Cooking time **26–28 minutes**

25 g (1 oz) whole **blanched almonds**

2 tablespoons **icing sugar**

75 g (3 oz) **white chocolate**, finely grated

8 soft **dates**, pitted and chopped

25 g (1 oz) **flaked almonds**, lightly toasted

8 slices **brioche**, buttered on both sides

50 ml (2 fl oz) **double cream**, whipped

Put the blanched almonds in a colander and sprinkle with a little cold water. Shake off any excess water and place the almonds on a nonstick baking sheet. Sift the icing sugar over the top and bake in a preheated oven, 180°C (350°F), Gas Mark 4, for about 20 minutes until they have crystallized.

Remove the almonds from the oven and set aside to cool, then put them in a freezer bag and tap lightly with a rolling pin until they are crushed but not powdery.

Mix together the grated chocolate, dates and almonds. Spoon the mixture on to 4 slices of the buttered brioche and top with the remaining slices to make 4 sandwiches.

Heat a griddle over a medium heat and cook the brioche sandwiches for 3–4 minutes. Turn them over and cook the other side for another 3–4 minutes to make a panini.

Cut the panini in half diagonally and serve immediately with whipped cream and sprinkled with crushed almonds.

For eggy bread, substitute the brioche for sweet French toasts. Dip each French toast in a mixture of 2 eggs lightly beaten with 4 tablespoons milk. Fry in butter, turning, until golden both sides. Omit the nuts and cream and serve with honey or syrup.

peach & blueberry crunch

Serves **4**
Preparation time **8 minutes**
Cooking time **8–10 minutes**

25 g (1 oz) **ground hazelnuts**
25 g (1 oz) **ground almonds**
25 g (1 oz) **caster sugar**
25 g (1 oz) **breadcrumbs**
410 g (13½ oz) can **peaches in natural juice**
125 g (4 oz) **blueberries**
150 ml (¼ pint) **double cream**
seeds from 1 **vanilla pod**
1 tablespoon **icing sugar**, sifted

Gently cook the ground nuts in a large frying pan with the sugar and breadcrumbs, stirring constantly until golden. Remove from the heat and leave to cool.

Put the peaches in a food processor or blender and blend with enough of the peach juice to make a thick, smooth purée.

Fold the blueberries gently into the purée and spoon into 4 glasses or individual serving dishes. Set aside some of the blueberries to decorate.

Whip the cream with the vanilla seeds and icing sugar until thick but not stiff and spoon evenly over the peach purée. When the crunchy topping is cool, sprinkle it over the blueberry mixture, top with the remaining blueberries and serve.

For apple & blackberry biscuit crunch, peel 450 g (14½ oz) cooking apples and cook with 2–3 tablespoons sugar and 2 tablespoons water. Fold 125 g (4 oz) blackberries into the apple purée and continue as above, but instead of breadcrumbs, use crushed digestive biscuits. Use the same amount and toast in the same way, but reduce the sugar to 1 tablespoon.

pancake stack with maple syrup

Serves **4**
Preparation time **10 minutes**
Cooking time **6 minutes**

1 **egg**
100 g (3½ oz) **strong plain flour**
125 ml (4 fl oz) **milk**
2½ tablespoons **vegetable oil**
1 tablespoon **caster sugar**
bottled **maple syrup**, to drizzle
8 scoops of **vanilla ice cream**

Put the egg, flour, milk, oil and sugar in a food processor or blender and whiz until smooth and creamy.

Heat a large frying pan over a medium heat and put in 4 half-ladlefuls of the batter to make 4 pancakes.

After about 1 minute the tops of the pancakes will start to set and air bubbles will rise to the top and burst. Use a spatula to turn the pancakes over and cook on the other side for 1 minute.

Repeat twice more until you have used all the batter and made 12 small pancakes in all.

Bring the pancakes to the table as a stack, drizzled with maple syrup, and serve 3 pancakes to each person, with scoops of ice cream.

For orange-flavoured pancakes, make a batter from 125 g (4 oz) plain flour, 2 teaspoons each caster sugar and grated orange rind, 1 teaspoon each cream of tartar and golden syrup, ½ teaspoon each salt and bicarbonate of soda, 1 egg, 125 ml (4 fl oz) warm milk and a few drops of orange essence. Cook the pancakes as above.

quick white chocolate mousse

Serves **4**

Preparation time **5 minutes**,
   plus chilling

Cooking time **10 minutes**

125 g (4 oz) **caster sugar**

50 g (2 oz) **shelled
   pistachios**

200 g (7 oz) **white chocolate**,
   chopped

280 ml (9½ fl oz) **double
   cream**

Dissolve the sugar with 4 tablespoons water in a small pan over a low heat. Increase the heat and boil until it begins to caramelize. Tip in the pistachios and stir, then pour the mixture on to some greaseproof paper on a baking sheet and leave to set.

Put the chocolate in a heatproof bowl. Heat the cream in a pan until it reaches boiling point, then remove from the heat and pour directly over the chocolate, stirring constantly until it has melted. Refrigerate until cold, then beat with a hand-held electric whisk until thick.

Spoon the cold chocolate into serving dishes, decorate with broken shards of the pistachio praline and serve.

For dark chocolate & orange mousse, substitute the white chocolate for plain dark chocolate, add ¼ teaspoon orange essence to the melted chocolate and use chopped walnuts instead of pistachios in the praline.

drunken orange slices

Serves **4**
Preparation time **10 minutes**
Cooking time **12 minutes**

4 large sweet **oranges**
50 g (2 oz) **soft brown sugar**
3 tablespoons **Cointreau**
2 tablespoons **whisky**
juice of 1 small **orange**
1 **vanilla pod**, split
1 **cinnamon stick**
4 **cloves**
2–3 blades of **mace** (optional)
ginger ice cream, to serve

Cut off the base and the top of the oranges. Cut down around the curve of the orange to remove all the rind and pith, leaving just the orange flesh. Cut the flesh horizontally into 5 mm (¼ inch) slices and set aside.

Heat 50 ml (2 fl oz) water gently with the sugar, 2 tablespoons of the Cointreau, the whisky, orange juice, vanilla pod, cinnamon stick, cloves and mace (if used) until the sugar has dissolved. Increase the heat and boil rapidly for 5 minutes. Allow to cool slightly, but keep warm.

Heat a griddle pan over a high heat and quickly cook the orange slices for about 1 minute on each side until caramelized. Top with the remaining Cointreau and set alight. Once the flames have died down, arrange the orange slices on serving dishes and drizzle with the orange syrup.

Serve the orange slices immediately with some ginger ice cream.

For non-alcoholic orange slices, slice 6 oranges as above and arrange them in a dish. Cut away the pith from the rind and finely slice the rind. Put it in a saucepan with just enough water to cover. Bring to the boil then immediately refresh in cold water. Place the rind in a clean pan, cover with water and simmer for 25 minutes. Dissolve 175 g (6 oz) caster sugar in 150 ml (¼ pint) water, boil for a few minutes and stir in 2 tablespoons lemon juice. Add the drained rind and pour over the sliced oranges. Chill, then serve with ice cream.

chocolate overload

Serves **4**

Preparation time **8 minutes**

8 **chocolate cream sandwich biscuits**, crushed

25 g (1 oz) **butter**, melted

500 ml (17 fl oz) tub softened **chocolate cookie ice cream**

2 tablespoons **runny caramel** or **dulce de leche** (optional)

white chocolate shavings, to decorate

milk chocolate shavings, to decorate

Mix the crushed biscuits with the melted butter and press firmly into the base of 4 dessert dishes.

Scoop the ice cream over the top of the biscuit base. Drizzle with the caramel or spoon over the dulce de leche (if used) and decorate with white and milk chocolate shavings. Serve immediately.

For chocolate sundaes with raspberries, replace the biscuits with 20 mini meringues and omit the butter. Layer the ice cream, meringues and 200 g (7 oz) raspberries in glasses. Drizzle with single cream and top with grated chocolate.

figs with yogurt & honey

Serves **4**
Preparation time **5 minutes**
Cooking time **10 minutes**

8 ripe **figs**
4 tablespoons **natural yogurt**
2 tablespoons **clear honey**

Slice the figs in half and place on a hot griddle pan, skin-side down. Sear for 10 minutes until the skins begin to blacken, then remove.

Arrange the figs on 4 plates and serve with a spoonful of yogurt and some honey spooned over the top.

For brioche French toasts with figs, yogurt & honey, brush 4 slices brioche with a mixture of 50 g (2 oz) melted butter and 50 ml (2 fl oz) cream and toast under a grill. Top with figs, as above.

nutty cinnamon risotto

Serves **4**
Preparation time **5 minutes**
Cooking time **25 minutes**

50 g (2 oz) **pecan nuts**
50 g (2 oz) **hazelnuts**
50 g (2 oz) **butter**
125 g (4 oz) **risotto rice**
5 teaspoons **soft brown sugar**
1 teaspoon **ground cinnamon**
600 ml (1 pint) hot **milk**

Heat a frying pan over a medium heat and dry-fry the nuts until golden. Remove and set aside.

Melt the butter in a medium saucepan, add the rice and cook, stirring, for 1 minute.

Stir 4 teaspoons of the sugar and the cinnamon into the hot milk, then start adding the milk to the rice, adding a little more once each addition has been absorbed. This should take about 20 minutes, when the rice should be soft but still with a little bite.

Spoon the risotto into serving bowls.

Blitz the nuts in a food processor with the remaining teaspoon of sugar, then sprinkle the mix over the top of risotto. Serve immediately.

For apricot, citrus & almond risotto, replace the pecan nuts with 100 g (3½ oz) chopped ready-to-eat dried apricots, and the hazelnuts with 100 g (3½ oz) toasted almonds and 2 tablespoons chopped Italian mixed peel.

blood-orange sorbet

Serves **4–6**
Preparation time **25 minutes**,
   plus chilling and freezing
Cooking time **about**
   20 minutes

250 g (8 oz) **caster sugar**
pared rind of 2 **blood**
   oranges
300 ml (½ pint) **blood orange**
   juice
chilled **Campari**, to serve
   (optional)
orange rind, to decorate

Heat the sugar over a low heat in a small saucepan with 250 ml (8 fl oz) water, stirring occasionally until completely dissolved.

Add the orange rind and increase the heat. Without stirring, boil the syrup for about 12 minutes and then set aside to cool completely.

When it is cold, strain the sugar syrup over the orange juice and stir together. Refrigerate for about 2 hours until really cold.

Pour the chilled orange syrup into an ice cream machine and churn for about 10 minutes. When the sorbet is almost frozen, scrape it into a plastic container and put it in the freezer compartment for a further hour until completely frozen. Alternatively, pour the chilled orange syrup into a shallow metal container and put it in the freezer for 2 hours. Remove and whisk with a hand-held electric whisk or balloon whisk, breaking up all the ice crystals. Return it to the freezer and repeat this process every hour or so until frozen.

Serve scoops of sorbet with a splash of chilled Campari, if liked, and decorate with thin strips of orange rind.

For papaya & lime sorbet, dissolve 125 g (4 oz) caster sugar in 150 ml (¼ pint) water. Boil for 5 minutes, then set aside to cool. Deseed, peel and dice the flesh of 1 ripe papaya. Process the papaya with the cooled sugar syrup. Stir in the grated rind and juice of 2 limes, chill and proceed as above.

rhubarb & raspberry crumble

Serves **4**
Preparation time **10 minutes**
Cooking time **25 minutes**

200 g (7 oz) **plain flour**
pinch of **salt**
150 g (5 oz) **unsalted butter**
200 g (7 oz) **soft brown sugar**
500 g (1 lb) fresh or frozen **rhubarb** (thawed if frozen), sliced
125 g (4 oz) fresh or frozen **raspberries**
3 tablespoons **orange juice**
raspberry ripple ice cream, to serve

Put the flour and salt in a bowl, add the butter and rub in with the fingertips until the mixture resembles breadcrumbs. Stir in 150 g (5 oz) of the sugar.

Mix together the fruits, the remaining sugar and orange juice and tip into a buttered dish. Sprinkle over the topping and cook in a preheated oven, 200°C (400°F), Gas Mark 6, for about 25 minutes or until golden brown and bubbling.

Remove and serve hot with raspberry ripple ice cream.

For apple & blackberry crumble, substitute the rhubarb and raspberries for 450 g (14½ oz) apples, peeled and chopped, and 450 g (14½ oz) blackberries. You could also use 450 g (14½ oz) plums, stoned and quartered, and 4 peeled and thinly sliced ripe pears.

chocolate & raspberry soufflés

Serves **4**

Preparation time **10 minutes**

Cooking time **13–18 minutes**

100 g (3½ oz) **plain dark chocolate**

3 **eggs**, separated

50 g (2 oz) **self-raising flour**, sifted

40 g (1½ oz) **caster sugar**

150 g (5 oz) **raspberries**, plus extra to serve (optional)

icing sugar sifted, to decorate

Break the chocolate into squares and put them in a large heatproof bowl over a saucepan of simmering water. Leave until melted, then remove from the heat and allow to cool a little. Whisk in the egg yolks and fold in the flour.

Whisk the egg whites and caster sugar in a medium bowl until they form soft peaks. Beat a spoonful of the egg whites into the chocolate mixture to loosen it before gently folding in the rest.

Put the raspberries into 4 lightly greased ramekins, pour over the chocolate mixture and cook in a preheated oven, 190°C (375°F), Gas Mark 5, for 12–15 minutes until the soufflés have risen.

Sprinkle the soufflés with icing sugar and serve with extra raspberries, if liked.

For white chocolate & mango soufflés, substitute the plain dark chocolate with white chocolate and the raspberries with 1 mango, peeled, stoned, diced, and divided among the ramekins.

summer fruit crunch

Serves **4–6**
Preparation time **10 minutes**
Cooking time **20 minutes**

50 g (2 oz) **rolled oats**
½ teaspoon **ground cinnamon**
½ teaspoon **mixed spice**
pinch of **ground ginger**
15 g (½ oz) **butter**, melted
1 tablespoon **clear honey**
2 tablespoons **sultanas**
400 g (13 oz) mixed fresh or
    frozen **summer fruits**
50 g (2 oz) **icing sugar**, plus
    extra to garnish
2 tablespoons **crème de
    cassis**
½ teaspoon **vanilla extract**
1 tablespoon **flaked almonds**,
    toasted, to garnish

Mix the oats and spices with the melted butter and honey until well combined.

Press on to a baking sheet and cook in a preheated oven, 180°C (350°F), Gas Mark 4, for 20 minutes, turning once. Remove and leave to cool before mixing in the sultanas.

Meanwhile, put the summer fruits in a pan with the icing sugar and 1 tablespoon water. Warm over a medium-low heat, stirring occasionally, until the fruit begins to collapse. Remove from the heat and stir in the crème de cassis and vanilla extract.

Spoon the fruit into dishes and sprinkle over the crunchy topping. Garnish with the toasted almonds and a sprinkling of icing sugar. Serve immediately.

For autumn plum crunch, stone and quarter 500 g (1 lb) plums and use instead of the summer fruits. Cook the plums in 100 ml (3½ fl oz) apple juice until just tender. Substitute the crème de cassis for sloe gin. Spoon into the dishes and finish as above.

baked lemon custards

Serves **4**

Preparation time **10 minutes**,
  plus infusing

Cooking time **about 1 hour**

12 **bay leaves**, bruised

2 tablespoons finely grated
  lemon rind

100 ml (3½ fl oz) **double
  cream**

4 **eggs**, plus 1 **egg yolk**

150 g (5 oz) **caster sugar**

100 ml (3½ fl oz) **lemon juice**

Put the bay leaves, lemon rind and cream in a small saucepan and heat gently until it reaches boiling point. Remove immediately from the heat and set aside for 2 hours to infuse.

Whisk together the eggs, egg yolk and sugar until the mixture is pale and creamy, then whisk in the lemon juice. Strain the cream mixture through a fine sieve into the egg mixture and stir until combined. Set aside 4 bay leaves for decoration.

Pour the custard into 4 individual ramekins and place on a baking sheet. Cook in a preheated oven, 120°C (250°F), Gas Mark ½, for 50 minutes or until the custards are almost set in the middle. Leave to stand until cold, then chill until required. Allow to return to room temperature before serving, decorated with the reserved bay leaves.

For plain baked custard, mix 1 tablespoon caster sugar with 1 egg, 150 ml (¼ pint) warm milk and a pinch of salt. Use the mixture to fill 1 flan case or 12 small pastry cases made from 250 g (8 oz) shortcrust pastry, pricked and baked blind in a preheated oven, 200°C (400°F), Gas Mark 6, for 20–25 minutes. Sprinkle over grated nutmeg and bake in a preheated oven, 200°C (400°F), Gas Mark 6, for about 20 minutes.

hot brioche with chocolate sauce

Serves **4**
Preparation time **5 minutes**
Cooking time **12 minutes**

100 g (3½ oz) **plain dark chocolate**
1 tablespoon **golden syrup**
125 g (4 oz) **butter**
4 tablespoons **double cream**
4 thick slices **brioche**
100 g (3½ oz) **demerara sugar**
4 scoops **vanilla** or **praline ice cream**
2 tablespoons **flaked almonds**, lightly toasted

Put the chocolate in a small saucepan with the golden syrup, 25 g (1 oz) of the butter and the cream and heat, stirring occasionally, until shiny and melted.

Meanwhile, melt the remaining butter and brush it over the brioche slices. Sprinkle over the sugar.

Heat a large frying pan over a low heat and cook the brioche slices in the pan for 3–4 minutes on each side until golden and crispy.

Serve hot, with a scoop of ice cream, the warm chocolate sauce and a scattering of nuts.

For quick ice cream brioche, serve 4 individual brioches cut in half and arranged on 4 dessert plates with a scoop of chocolate ice cream, whipped cream and a scattering of roughly chopped chocolate chips.

upside-down grapefruit cakes

Serves **6**
Preparation time **15 minutes**
Cooking time **about
40 minutes**

1 **grapefruit**, peeled and cut
into 6 thin slices
6 tablespoons **golden syrup**
175 g (6 oz) **unsalted butter**,
at room temperature
275 g (9 oz) **soft brown
sugar**
2 **eggs**
175 g (6 oz) **self-raising flour**
pinch of **salt**
finely grated rind of 1 **lime**
2 tablespoons **grapefruit
juice**
2–3 tablespoons **milk**

Push a slice of grapefruit to the base of each of
6 buttered pudding moulds or ramekins and drizzle
with a tablespoon of golden syrup. Set aside.

Cream together the butter and sugar until light and
fluffy. Add the eggs, one at a time, beating well until
incorporated. Gently fold in the flour, salt and lime rind,
then fold in the grapefruit juice and milk so that the
mixture has a good dropping consistency.

Spoon the mixture into the moulds or ramekins and
smooth down.

Put the moulds in a large roasting tin half-filled with
boiling water and cook in a preheated oven, 180°C
(350°F), Gas Mark 4, for about 40 minutes or until
risen and golden.

Remove the cakes from the oven, lift them out of the
hot water and leave to cool for 5 minutes. Loosen the
sides of the cakes by running a knife around the inside
of the moulds and then turn them out into serving
bowls. Serve immediately with cream.

For crème anglaise to serve as an accompaniment
for a special occasion, heat 475 ml (16 fl oz) milk with
a split vanilla pod to boiling point. Remove from the
heat. Beat together 6 egg yolks and 125 g (4 oz)
caster sugar, then slowly beat in the hot milk. Return
to the heat and stir continuously until the custard
thickens. Remove the vanilla pod and serve.

muffin trifle with boozy berries

Serves **4**

Preparation time **15 minutes**

400 g (13 oz) fresh **mixed berries**, such as strawberries, redcurrants and raspberries, plus extra to decorate

3 tablespoons **crème de cerises** or **cherry brandy**

1 tablespoon **maple syrup**

2 large **blueberry muffins**, sliced

150 ml (¼ pint) **double cream**, whipped to soft peaks

Put the fruit in a bowl and use the back of a fork to crush it with the cherry liqueur or brandy and maple syrup until well combined.

Arrange the sliced muffins in the bottom of a glass dish. Spoon over the fruit and top with the whipped cream. Decorate with the extra berries and serve.

For Black Forest trifle, slice 1 chocolate Swiss roll and arrange in the bottom of a glass dish. Substitute the mixed berries for stoned black cherries. Scrape the seeds of a vanilla pod into the double cream before whipping. Finish as above.

chocolate orange brownies

Makes **16**
Preparation time **15–20
  minutes**
Cooking time **30–35 minutes**

250 g (8 oz) **orange-
  flavoured chocolate** or
  plain dark chocolate with
  1 teaspoon **orange essence**
250 g (8 oz) **unsalted butter**
150 g (5 oz) **caster sugar**
4 **eggs**
finely grated rind of
  1 **orange**
175 g (6 oz) **plain flour**
pinch of **salt**
1 teaspoon **baking powder**
150 g (5 oz) **milk chocolate**,
  roughly chopped
75 g (3 oz) **macadamia nuts**,
  roughly chopped

Put the chocolate and butter in a heavy-based saucepan over a very low heat and stir until both ingredients are just melted. Remove from the heat, stir in the sugar and set aside to cool a little.

Pour the chocolate mixture into a large bowl and beat in the eggs, orange rind and orange essence (if used).

Sift the flour, salt and baking powder into the bowl and fold in, together with the chocolate chunks and macadamia nuts.

Pour the mixture into a greased and lined cake tin, about 20 x 30 x 5 cm (8 x 12 x 2 inches).

Cook in a preheated oven, 180°C (350°F), Gas Mark 4, for 25–30 minutes or until set but not too firm. Leave the brownie to cool in the tin, then cut it into squares and serve.

For ginger chocolate brownies, use plain dark chocolate (not orange-flavoured chocolate) and omit the orange rind. Instead, add 1 tablespoon ground ginger to the flour and 50 g (2 oz) chopped glacé ginger to the chocolate.

apple & sultana pot

Serves **4**
Preparation time **15 minutes**
Cooking time **15–23 minutes**

2 **lapsang souchong tea bags**
1 tablespoon **clear honey**
3 tablespoons **sultanas**
3 dessert or cooking **apples**, peeled, cored and diced
½ teaspoon **mixed spice**
25 g (1 oz) **dark brown sugar**
25 g (1 oz) **unsalted butter**
150 g (5 oz) **double cream**, whipped to soft peaks
caster sugar, as required
ginger snaps, to serve

Make a strong infusion of tea using the tea bags in 100 ml (3½ fl oz) boiling water. Stir in the honey and sultanas and set aside to infuse.

Put the apples in a saucepan with the mixed spice, brown sugar and butter. Remove the teabags from the infusion and pour the liquid over the apples.

Cover and cook over a medium-low heat, stirring frequently, for 15–20 minutes until the apples start to collapse. Crush to a chunky purée.

Stir the double cream into the apple purée until well combine, then spoon the mixture into 4 individual ovenproof dishes.

Sprinkle the surface generously with caster sugar, then place the dishes under a hot grill until the sugar begins to caramelize. Serve warm or cold with ginger snaps.

For raspberry & rosewater pots with ground almonds, use the back of a fork to lightly crush 250 g (8 oz) fresh raspberries with 2 tablespoons honey. Stir in 1 tablespoon rosewater and 3 tablespoons ground almonds. Spoon into 4 ramekin dishes and top each one with a generous tablespoon whipped cream before sprinkling with caster sugar and caramelizing as above.

croissants with chestnut cream

Serves **4**
Preparation time **15 minutes**
Cooking time **2–3 minutes**

75 g (3 oz) **unsalted butter**,
  melted
4 day-old **croissants**, split in
  half horizontally
4 teaspoons **muscovado**
  sugar
125 ml (4 fl oz) **sweetened**
  chestnut purée
125 ml (4 fl oz) **mascarpone**
  cheese
2 tablespoons **natural yogurt**
1 tablespoon **clear honey**,
  plus extra for drizzling

To serve
chopped **marrons glacés**
  (optional)
crushed **chocolate-covered**
  coffee beans (optional)

Brush the melted butter over the cut sides of the croissants, then sprinkle them with the sugar. Set aside.

Beat the chestnut purée with the mascarpone, yogurt and honey until smooth.

Heat a griddle pan over a low heat and cook the croissants gently, cut-side down, for 2–3 minutes until hot and golden.

Transfer the croissants to serving plates, top with some of the chestnut cream and drizzle with a little extra honey. Sprinkle with a few chopped marrons glacés or crushed chocolate coffee beans, if liked, and serve immediately.

For chocolate cream to serve as an alternative to chestnut cream, substitute the chestnut purée for 4 tablespoons chocolate spread and mix with the mascarpone and yogurt. Omit the honey. After cooking the croissants, spread them with apricot conserve and then with the chocolate cream.

pink grapefruit parfait

Serves **4**

Preparation time **15 minutes**

2 **pink grapefruit**

5 tablespoons **dark brown sugar**, plus extra for sprinkling

250 ml (8 fl oz) **double cream**

175 ml (6 fl oz) **Greek yogurt**

3 tablespoons **elderflower cordial**

½ teaspoon **ground ginger**

½ teaspoon **ground cinnamon**

brandy snaps, to serve (optional)

Finely grate the rind of 1 grapefruit, making sure you don't get any of the bitter white pith. Cut the skin and the white membrane off both grapefruit and cut between the membranes to remove the segments. Put them in a large dish, sprinkle with 2 tablespoons of the sugar and set aside.

Whisk together the cream and yogurt until thick but not stiff.

Fold in the elderflower cordial, spices, grapefruit rind and remaining sugar until smooth. Pour the mixture into attractive glasses, arranging the grapefruit segments between layers of parfait.

Sprinkle the top with sugar and serve immediately with brandy snaps, if liked.

For orange & blackcurrant parfait, replace the grapefruit with segments from 3 oranges and the elderflower cordial with blackcurrant cordial. Omit the ground ginger and serve sprinkled with chocolate shavings.

sweet chestnut mess

Serves **4**
Preparation time **15 minutes**

250 g (8 oz) **fromage frais**
1 tablespoon **icing sugar**,
    sifted
100 g (3½ oz) **sweetened
    chestnut purée**
100 g (3½ oz) **meringues**,
    crushed
dark chocolate shards cut
    from a bar, to decorate

Beat the fromage frais with the icing sugar. Stir in half the chestnut purée and the crushed meringues.

Spoon the remaining chestnut purée into individual serving dishes and top with the meringue mess. Decorate with the dark chocolate shards and serve.

For sweet chestnut pancakes, stir the chestnut purée into the fromage frais. Heat 8 ready-made pancakes according to the instructions on the packet and spread them with the chestnut purée mix. Roll them up and sprinkle with cocoa and icing sugar .

lemon drizzle cake

Serves **8**
Preparation time **20 minutes**
Cooking time **22–28 minutes**

5 **eggs**
100 g (3½ oz) **caster sugar**
pinch of **salt**
125 g (4 oz) **plain flour**
1 teaspoon **baking powder**
finely grated rind of 1 **lemon**
1 tablespoon **lemon juice**
100 g (3½ oz) **butter**, melted
  and cooled
crème fraîche or **soured
  cream**, to serve

Syrup
250 g (8 oz) **icing sugar**
125 ml (4 fl oz) **lemon juice**
finely grated rind of 1 **lemon**
seeds scraped from 1 **vanilla
  pod**

Put the eggs, sugar and salt in a large heatproof
bowl set over a pan of barely simmering water.
Beat the mixture with a hand-held electric whisk for
2–3 minutes or until it triples in volume and thickens
to the consistency of lightly whipped cream. Remove
from the heat.

Sift in the flour and baking powder, add the lemon
rind and juice and drizzle the butter down the sides
of the bowl. Fold in gently, pour into a greased and
lined 22 cm (8½ inch) square cake tin and cook in
a preheated oven, 180°C (350°F), Gas Mark 4, for
20–25 minutes or until risen, golden and coming away
from the sides of the tin.

Meanwhile, put all the ingredients for the syrup in a
small pan and heat gently until the sugar has dissolved.
Increase the heat and boil rapidly for 4–5 minutes.
Set aside to cool a little.

Remove the cake from the oven, leave it to rest for
5 minutes, then make holes over the surface with a
skewer. Drizzle over two-thirds of the warm syrup.
Leave the cake to cool and absorb the syrup.

Remove the cake from the tin and peel away the lining
paper. Place the cake on a dish and serve in squares
or slices with a heaped spoonful of crème fraîche or
soured cream and an extra drizzle of syrup.

For citrus drizzle cake with sorbet, use orange rind
and juice instead of lemon and serve topped with
lemon sorbet.

passion fruit yogurt fool

Serves **4**

Preparation time **8 minutes**

6 **passion fruit**, halved, flesh
   and seeds removed
300 ml (½ pint) **Greek yogurt**
1 tablespoon **clear honey**
200 ml (7 fl oz) **whipping
   cream**, whipped to soft
   peaks
4 pieces of **shortbread**,
   to serve

Stir the passion fruit flesh and seeds into the yogurt
with the honey.

Fold the cream into the yogurt. Spoon into tall glasses
and serve with the shortbread.

For mango & lime yogurt fool, omit the passion fruit,
instead puréeing 1 large ripe peeled and stoned mango
with the zest of 1 lime and icing sugar to taste. Mix into
the yogurt and fold in the cream. Omit the honey.

mint choc chip cheesecake

Serves **4–6**
Preparation time **12 minutes**, plus setting

200 g (7 oz) **chocolate biscuits**
100 g (3½ oz) **mint-flavoured dark chocolate**, chopped
50 g (2 oz) **butter**, melted
200 g (7 oz) **cream cheese**
200 g (7 oz) **mascarpone cheese**
50 g (2 oz) **caster sugar**
1 tablespoon **crème de menthe** or **peppermint extract**
2 drops **green food colouring**
50 g (2 oz) **plain dark chocolate chips**

Put the biscuits and chocolate in a food processor or blender and process to make fine crumbs. Mix with the melted butter and press the mixture gently over the base of a 20 cm (8 inch), round, springform cake tin. Place in the freezer to set while making the cream cheese mixture.

Beat together the cream cheese, mascarpone, sugar, mint liqueur or extract and food colouring in a large bowl. Stir in 40 g (1½ oz) of the chocolate chips and spoon the mixture over the biscuit base, smoothing with the back of a spoon.

Place in the refrigerator to chill for about 1 hour.

Loosen the edge with a knife, then remove the cheesecake from the tin carefully. Scatter over the remaining chocolate chips, roughly chopped.

For individual ginger cake cheesecakes, use 4 x 7.5 cm (3 inch) fluted tartlet tins. Make a base for each cheesecake by pressing a slice of ginger cake inside each tin. Replace the mint liqueur with ginger wine.

index

acknowledgements

Executive Editor: Nicky Hill
Editor: Camilla Davis
Executive Art Editor: Penny Stock
Designer: Grade
Photographer: Stephen Conroy
Home Economist: Joanna Farrow
Prop Stylist: Liz Hippisley
Production Manager: Martin Croshaw

Special photography: © Octopus Publishing Group Limited/Stephen Conroy. **Other photography:** © Octopus Publishing Group Ltd/Gareth Sambridge 29, 39, 49, 101, 123, 153, 187, 191, 195, 199, 223; /Gus Filgate 24, 117, 129, 147; /Lis Parsons 33, 57, 63, 73, 107, 113, 120, 137, 141, 163, 179, 203, 211, 215, 219, 225; /Stephen Conroy 21, 57, 99; /William Lingwood 19, 97, 233; /William Reavell 159.